Trusts in 30 Days

Independently Published
Fort Lauderdale, Florida
https://www.amazon.com/author/woodyclermont

Trusts in 30 Days

A Practical Guide to Protecting Assets and Planning for the Future

Woody R. Clermont

First Edition
October 5, 2025

Legal and Tax Disclaimer: This book is for educational and informational purposes only. It does not constitute legal, tax, accounting, or financial advice, and no attorney–client or other professional relationship is created by reading it. Trust and estate laws vary by state and change over time; consult a qualified attorney and tax professional in your jurisdiction before taking action. The author and publisher disclaim any liability for actions taken or not taken based on this work.

Trademarks: Product and company names mentioned herein may be trademarks of their respective owners. Use of such names is for identification only and does not imply endorsement.

Library of Congress Control Number (LCCN): LCCN Pending

Cover design: The Unrelenting Alchemist

Interior design: Woody R. Clermont

Printed in the United States of America

Independently Published, Fort Lauderdale, Florida

"Love is very dangerous if you just have love and don't have the ability to be lovable."

— Dick Gregory

Acknowledgments

Thank you to the people who made this book possible: You know who you are. Your insights and encouragement sharpened the guidance and kept the focus on clarity for everyday readers. Thank you Scheril, for always pushing me to be my best. Thank you to my daughter Nubia and my son Devon. You light up my world.

How to Use This Book

This guide is designed to get you from zero to a working, funded trust in 30 days. Each chapter ends with a short checklist. If you already have a will or some planning in place, skim Chapters 1–3, then focus on Chapters 6-8, 10, and 17 for setup and the 30-day plan. Keep notes, confirm state-specific rules, and involve a professional whenever you hit a gray area.

Permissions and Requests

To request permission to quote, reproduce charts or checklists, or adapt materials from this book, please email wclermont2004@gmail.com. For speaking, bulk orders, or instructor copies, visit https://www.amazon.com/author/woodyclermont.

Contents

Acknowledgments vii

How to Use This Book ix

Permissions and Requests xi

1 Why Trusts Matter 1
- 1.1 The Core Idea 2
- 1.2 Why Trusts Are Popular 4
- 1.3 Dispelling the Myths 6
- 1.4 When a Will is Not Enough 8
- 1.5 Peace of Mind 9
- 1.6 Takeaway 10

2 Players in a Trust 11
- 2.1 The Grantor (or Settlor) 12
- 2.2 The Trustee 14
- 2.3 The Beneficiaries 15
- 2.4 Successor Trustees and Backups 17
- 2.5 How the Roles Work Together 19
- 2.6 Takeaway 20

3 The Grantor 21
- 3.1 Why the Grantor Matters 21

3.2 Names and Terminology 22
3.3 Core Powers of the Grantor 22
3.4 Responsibilities of the Grantor 24
3.5 The Grantor During Life 24
3.6 The Grantor at Incapacity 25
3.7 The Grantor at Death 25
3.8 Common Mistakes Grantors Make 25
3.9 Case Studies 26
3.10 Checklist for Grantors 27
3.11 Takeaway 28

4 Trustees 29
4.1 Why Trustees Matter 29
4.2 Who Can Serve as Trustee 30
4.3 How Trustees Are Replaced 33
4.4 Core Fiduciary Duties 35
4.5 Distribution Standards 37
4.6 First 90 Days Checklist 39
4.7 Investments and Risk 43
4.8 Taxes and Reporting 45
4.9 Compensation & Expenses 46
4.10 Communication 47
4.11 Problem Spots 49
4.12 Advanced Tools 50
4.13 Special Asset Playbook 50
4.14 Case Studies 51
4.15 Trustee Boundaries 52
4.16 Key Takeaways 53

5 The Beneficiaries 54
5.1 Who Are Beneficiaries? 54
5.2 Rights of Beneficiaries 56

5.3 Expectations and Realities 57
5.4 Special Types 59
5.5 Common Problems 60
5.6 Case Studies 61
5.7 Checklist 62
5.8 Practical Toolkit 63
5.9 Takeaway 64

6 Estate Planning 65
6.1 A Starting Point 66
6.2 A Living Document 77
6.3 Other Planning Tools 84
6.4 Why Trusts? 86
6.5 Checklist 87
6.6 Takeaway 88

7 Living Trust 89
7.1 Step One: Decide 90
7.2 Step Two: Draft 92
7.3 Step Three: Fund 94
7.4 Step Four: Store 95
7.5 Common Pitfalls 96
7.6 Step Five: Maintain 97
7.7 Takeaway 98

8 Uses of Trusts 99
8.1 Probate Avoidance 100
8.2 Protecting Children 101
8.3 Blended Families 102
8.4 Planning for Incapacity 103
8.5 Takeaway 104

9 Taxes and Trusts 105

9.1 Key Concepts 106
9.2 What Changes 107
9.3 Taxes 109
9.4 Lifetime Transfers 110
9.5 Income Taxes 111
9.6 Basis at Death 113
9.7 Help? 114
9.8 Takeaway 115

10 Common Mistakes 116
10.1 Forgetting to Fund 117
10.2 Wrong Trustee 118
10.3 DIY Pitfalls 119
10.4 Failing to Update 120
10.5 Mismatches 120
10.6 Overlooking Taxes 121
10.7 Too Vague 121
10.8 Co-Trustee Chaos 122
10.9 Real Estate Headaches 122
10.10 No Plan 122
10.11 Digital Assets 123
10.12 Paperwork Gaps 123
10.13 Three Fast Lessons 124
10.14 Other Overlooked Mistakes 124
10.15 Takeaway 125

11 Florida Trusts 126
11.1 Florida Trust Law 126
11.2 Trusts in Florida 127
11.3 Funding and Title Issues 128
11.4 Duties 129
11.5 Spousal Rights 130

11.6 Creditor Claims 130
11.7 Notice of Obligations 131
11.8 Contests and Deadlines 131
11.9 Directed Trusts 131
11.10 Income Rules 132
11.11 Nuts and Bolts 133
11.12 Common Florida Pitfalls 133
11.13 Practical Checklist 134
11.14 Closing Thought 135

12 Guardianships 136
12.1 What Is Guardianship? 137
12.2 Why Guardianships Exist 137
12.3 Comparison 138
12.4 Directives 139
12.5 Guardianship vs. Trusts 139
12.6 Life Estates 140
12.7 Other Advance Directives 141
12.8 Practical Examples 141
12.9 Still Necessary 142
12.10 Takeaway 142

13 Real Property 144
13.1 Acquire Property 145
13.2 Estates in Land 146
13.3 Concurrent Ownership 148
13.4 Statutory Spousal Rights 149
13.5 Related Doctrines 150
13.6 Title and Recordation 151
13.7 Medicaid Planning 152
13.8 Lending Issues 152
13.9 Common-Interest Ownerships 153

13.10 Rule Against Perpetuities 154
13.11 Takeaway 154

14 Power of Attorney 156
14.1 Attorney-in-Fact 157
14.2 Types of Powers of Attorney 158
14.3 Powers Granted 159
14.4 Limits of a POA 160
14.5 Other Planning Tools 161
14.6 Practical Applications 162
14.7 Risks and Abuse 163
14.8 Florida-Specific 164
14.9 Takeaway 164

15 Revocable Living Trust Form 166
15.1 The Form 166
15.2 Sample 174
15.3 Schedule A — Trust Property 179

16 Irrevocable Living Trust Form 180

17 Trust Revocation Form 185

18 Living Trust Amendment Form 189

19 Special Needs Trust Template 193

20 Pet Trust Form 199

21 Last Will & Testament with Pour-Over Will 205

22 Advance Healthcare Directive / Living Will 211

23 Durable Power of Attorney 216

24 Minor Child Medical Consent Form 221

25 HIPAA Authorization Form 226

26 Financial Information Release Authorization 231

27 Guardian Nomination Form 236

28 Beneficiary Designation Form 241

29 Memorandum of Personal Property 245

30 Letter of Intent 249

31 Digital Assets Authorization Form 253

32 Funeral and Burial Instructions Form 258

33 Business Succession Plan Template 263

34 Designation of Standby Guardian 268

35 Special Power of Attorney for Childcare 273

36 Working with Lawyers 278

36.1 When DIY is Fine vs. When It's Risky . 279
36.2 Shopping for an Attorney 280
36.3 Online Kits and Red Flags 282
36.4 The Hybrid Approach 283
36.5 Beyond the Basics 284
36.6 Case Examples 284
36.7 Takeaway 285

37 Miscellaneous Topics **287**
37.1 Bulletproof Living Trusts 288
37.2 Seven Deadly Mistakes 288
37.3 Minimizing Taxes 289
37.4 Asset Protection Strategies 290
37.5 Out of Probate 290
37.6 Funding Trusts Correctly 291
37.7 Charitable Giving 291
37.8 Updating Your Plan 292
37.9 Building Blocks 292
37.10 Incapacity 293
37.11 Digital Asset Protection 293
37.12 Cross-Border Planning 293
37.13 Special Needs 294
37.14 Business Succession 294
37.15 Assembling the Team 295
37.16 Guiding Estate Administration 295
37.17 Takeaway 296

38 30-Day Plan **297**
38.1 Clerks, Judges, and Reality 298
38.2 Dealing with Other Entities 299
38.3 Week 1 301
38.4 Week 2 302
38.5 Week 3 304
38.6 Week 4 305
38.7 Checklist 306
38.8 Takeaway 307

Chapter 1

Why Trusts Matter

Most people first hear the word "trust" and immediately picture old-money families with sprawling estates, country club memberships, or labyrinthine tax maneuvers. Hollywood doesn't help—terms like "trust fund baby" make it sound as though trusts exist only to bankroll luxury cars or exotic vacations for heirs who never worked a day in their lives. In reality, nothing could be further from the truth. A trust is not inherently a symbol of wealth; it is a structure. It is, in essence, a legal container designed to hold your property. What makes it powerful is not just the property inside but the rules you attach to it—rules about who manages it, who benefits, and under what circumstances.

Think of it this way: you already use containers in daily life. A bank account contains your money and applies rules about deposits and withdrawals. A deed is a container that captures your ownership of a house. A will is a container for your instructions about what happens after you die. A trust is another container—but unlike the others, it is designed to keep working even if you cannot. Where a bank account sits idle without your password, or a deed requires court oversight after your death, a trust stays alive, humming quietly in the background, carrying out your instructions seamlessly. That continuity is what makes it such a powerful planning tool for ordinary people, not just the ultra-wealthy.

1.1 The Core Idea

At its core, a trust is nothing more than an agreement. But within that simplicity lies enormous flexibility. You, the creator—often called the grantor or settlor—decide to take property that belongs to you and place it inside this legal container. You then appoint a trustee, the person or institution responsible for managing the trust according to the rules you set. Finally, you name beneficiaries: the people or organizations who will eventually receive the benefit of what you placed inside.

That's the entire skeleton. Grantor, trustee, beneficiaries. Yet with those three players, you can create an arrangement that stretches across decades. For example, you might create a trust today that allows you to remain in control of your house and savings while you are alive and well. But if you become ill, your successor trustee can step in to pay bills or handle property without missing a beat. After you pass, your children or grandchildren may inherit under carefully written conditions—perhaps at certain ages, or for specific purposes like education or medical needs.

Trusts as Blueprints

The trust document functions like a blueprint. Just as an architect's plan dictates where the walls go and how the plumbing runs, the trust lays out exactly how your assets should be handled, both during your life and after your death. Unlike a one-page will, which often requires heavy lifting by courts and lawyers, a trust can operate smoothly and privately, without dragging your family into years of paperwork and court hearings. A good blueprint anticipates not only the house's beauty but also its storms, earthquakes, and repairs. So too does a trust anticipate incapacity, disputes, or changing family dynamics.

Historical Roots

Trusts are not a modern gimmick. They trace back to medieval England, when knights leaving for the Crusades entrusted their land to friends to manage for their families. Courts recognized these arrangements, and the concept of the "use" evolved into the modern trust. Across centuries, the basic need has not changed: people want a way to protect and transfer property without chaos. Trusts answered then, and still answer now.

1.2 Why Trusts Are Popular

Why do so many people choose to create a trust? Because it solves real, practical problems that nearly every family faces. A will is a static instruction sheet. A trust is dynamic, alive, and adaptable.

Four Core Advantages

- **Avoiding Probate.** Probate is the formal court process that validates a will and distributes assets. Even in the simplest cases, it often takes months, sometimes years, and comes with court costs and attorney's fees. A trust largely bypasses probate because the assets already belong to the trust, not to your estate. That means your loved ones can receive what you intended with less red tape.

- **Privacy.** Probate is a public proceeding. In many states, anyone can go to the courthouse and look up the file, seeing exactly who inherited what. That may not bother you, but for many families, keeping financial affairs private is a form of protection against gossip, opportunists, and even predators who target heirs. A trust does its work quietly, outside of the public eye.
- **Control.** Unlike a will, which makes a one-time distribution, a trust allows you to set rules that last for years. You can require that money be used only for education, that children inherit in stages (say, one-third at 25, one-third at 30, and the balance at 35), or that a trustee must approve expenses for health and housing. This level of control means you can protect your beneficiaries from their own inexperience, or from outside influences like creditors or ex-spouses.
- **Continuity.** Life rarely unfolds neatly. People fall ill, become incapacitated, or suffer accidents. A will does nothing until you die. A trust, however, is already in place, ready to function if you cannot. If you are hospitalized or in a coma, your successor trustee can immediately step in to pay your

mortgage, keep the lights on, or ensure that dependents are cared for—all without needing a court-appointed guardian.

Everyday Examples

- A single mother with a modest home places it in a trust, ensuring her children inherit without probate delay.
- An elderly couple names each other as co-trustees. When one suffers a stroke, the other continues managing their accounts without disruption.
- A young family sets conditions that their children can access funds for college, but not for frivolous spending at eighteen.

These benefits explain why families with even modest assets find trusts appealing. The point is not luxury—it is efficiency, privacy, and peace of mind.

1.3 Dispelling the Myths

One of the biggest obstacles to using trusts is the myth that they are only for millionaires. You may have heard the phrase "trust fund kid" and assumed the tool doesn't apply to you. The truth is, if you own a home, have savings, or have children, you are squarely in the category of people who can benefit.

Myth 1: Trusts are Only for the Wealthy

False. Probate costs consume proportionally more of small estates than large ones. Middle-class families often stand to gain the most.

Myth 2: Trusts are Overly Complicated

Also false. Once created, they often simplify life. A trustee follows instructions; no court oversight needed.

Myth 3: Trusts Always Save Taxes

Not true. Revocable trusts are tax-neutral during life. Special trusts may reduce taxes, but that is not their universal purpose.

Myth 4: Trusts are Too Expensive

Measured against probate costs, most trusts save money. A few hours with an attorney today can spare your heirs months of court battles.

1.4 When a Will is Not Enough

A will has its place. It names guardians for children, directs property at death, and provides clarity. But it is limited. It only speaks after death, and it always funnels property through probate.

Incapacity Gap

If you suffer a stroke and cannot manage your affairs, a will is silent. Your family may need to petition the court for guardianship to access accounts. A properly funded trust, by contrast, is already at work. Your successor trustee can step in without delay.

Distribution Problems

Even after death, a will can cause problems. It distributes property in one lump sum, which may not suit beneficiaries' needs. A trust allows staged or conditional distributions, protecting children from poor decisions or providing ongoing care for a disabled relative.

Case Example – The Will That Failed

A Florida retiree left only a will. His estate spent 18 months in probate. Court costs drained thousands, and his family endured public scrutiny. A simple trust would have spared them delay, expense, and exposure.

1.5 Peace of Mind

At the end of the day, the greatest value of a trust is the calm it brings. Families dealing with grief or crisis often find themselves overwhelmed by paperwork, waiting periods, and arguments over what the deceased "would have wanted." A trust eliminates much of that uncertainty. It provides a roadmap your family can follow with confidence.

It also reinforces a sense of stewardship. When you set up a trust, you are not just arranging finances—you are shaping how your loved ones will experience one of life's hardest transitions. That gift of clarity is immeasurable. For many, it is the single most compassionate act they can perform for their families.

Checklist: Peace of Mind in Practice

- Your heirs know exactly what happens next.
- The court is not involved unless absolutely necessary.
- Bills get paid without delay.

- Privacy is preserved.
- Conflicts are minimized.

The cost of creating a trust is almost always outweighed by the savings in money, time, and heartache that it prevents. A little planning today saves countless headaches tomorrow.

1.6 Takeaway

Trusts are not exotic creations reserved for the rich. They are practical, flexible, and deeply human tools for carrying your intentions forward. Whether you own a modest home, a retirement account, or a complex portfolio, a trust can streamline what happens when you cannot act for yourself. It is not about money—it is about clarity, efficiency, and care.

By the time you finish this book, you will know not just what a trust is, but how to build one, fund it, and keep it current. More importantly, you will have a 30-day plan to put everything in place. This is not theory. It is action. Within a month, you can go from uncertainty to confidence, knowing your affairs are in order and your family is protected.

Chapter 2

Players in a Trust

If a trust is a stage, the people involved are the cast. The script—the trust document—spells out the story, but without the actors, nothing happens. Understanding who the players are, what roles they perform, and how they interact is crucial to making your trust work. In this chapter, we will meet each of them: the grantor, the trustee, the beneficiaries, and the successors who step in when needed. Each role is simple in definition but carries real responsibilities and consequences. Cast the parts wisely, and the show will run smoothly for years. Cast them poorly, and the curtain may fall in confusion and conflict.

2.1 The Grantor (or Settlor)

Every trust begins with one person: the grantor. That's you, the person creating the trust. You decide what property to place in it, who will benefit, and what rules to write. The law may use different labels—settlor, trustor, trust maker—but they all mean the same thing: the origin point.

Being the grantor is not complicated, but it requires thoughtfulness. You are not just writing down names and numbers. You are shaping how your assets will flow for years to come. Imagine planting a tree. The way you choose the soil, the spacing, and the type of seed determines whether it grows straight and strong or bends under stress. As grantor, you set the foundation.

Responsibilities of the Grantor

- Selecting the type of trust (revocable, irrevocable, joint, etc.).
- Defining clear terms for distribution.
- Choosing trustees and successors.
- Ensuring assets are properly transferred into the trust.

Most living trusts are "revocable," meaning the grantor retains control during life. You can amend the terms, add property, remove property, or revoke the trust entirely. This flexibility makes the grantor role relatively light in day-to-day obligations but heavy in long-term vision. Your main job is to be clear about your goals and to express them in plain, workable instructions.

Case Study – The Thoughtful Grantor

A grandmother with three grandchildren created a trust that funded education expenses. She specified that "education" included trade schools, apprenticeships, and graduate programs. Because she thought carefully, her trust avoided disputes and supported her grandchildren's diverse paths.

Case Study – The Vague Grantor

Another man wrote only, "my children should be treated fairly." Without definitions, the trustee faced endless arguments over what "fair" meant—equal amounts, or weighted for need? His lack of precision sparked years of tension.

2.2 The Trustee

If the grantor is the architect, the trustee is the builder. The trustee manages the assets, carries out the rules, and keeps the trust running smoothly. This is not a ceremonial role. The trustee has legal duties—called fiduciary duties—to act in the best interest of the beneficiaries. That means no self-dealing, no shortcuts, and no ignoring the rules you wrote.

For a revocable living trust, you will likely serve as your own trustee while alive and healthy. That way, you stay in control. But you also name successor trustees, people who will step in if you die or become incapacitated. Choosing those successors wisely is one of the most important decisions you will make.

Qualities of a Good Trustee

- Organized and responsible.
- Honest and impartial.
- Comfortable with financial basics.
- Willing to seek professional advice when needed.

A bad trustee can drain an estate through neglect, poor recordkeeping, or outright misconduct. A good trustee preserves assets and keeps peace in the family.

Some people choose individuals—spouses, adult children, siblings. Others appoint institutions, like banks or trust companies, which offer professional management but also charge fees. There is no one-size-fits-all answer. The best trustee is the one who can follow instructions faithfully and balance fairness with firmness.

Case Study – The Capable Trustee

A son named trustee for his mother's trust worked with an accountant to handle taxes and distributed funds as directed. The process was smooth, and all siblings praised his fairness.

Case Study – The Problem Trustee

A cousin named as trustee refused to share information with beneficiaries, delayed distributions, and borrowed trust money. Eventually, a court removed him for breach of duty. The family suffered needlessly because the wrong person was chosen.

2.3 The Beneficiaries

Beneficiaries are the people (or organizations) for whose benefit the trust exists. They may be family, friends, or charities. They are the recipients of the trust's income or assets, either immediately or at some future point. In some cases, beneficiaries have current rights (for example, a spouse receiving income while alive), and in others they are contingent (children who inherit only after the spouse dies).

Beneficiaries are at the heart of potential conflict. Expectations may not match reality. One child may believe they are "owed" more than another. A charity may expect a larger gift. The trust document is designed to quiet these disputes by spelling out exactly what happens and when. But even the clearest instructions can cause tension if beneficiaries feel overlooked or confused. That is why communication, even during life, is often as important as the written terms.

Beneficiaries and Trustee Duties

Trustees must:

- Keep beneficiaries informed.
- Act impartially among multiple beneficiaries.
- Avoid favoritism or bias.
- Provide regular accounting when required.

When there are multiple beneficiaries—say, children of

different marriages—the trustee is walking a tightrope, balancing interests without letting the trust collapse into resentment.

Case Study – Cooperative Beneficiaries

Siblings who were all named equal beneficiaries agreed to wait for asset sales before taking distributions. Their cooperation allowed the trustee to maximize value.

Case Study – Combative Beneficiaries

In another family, one child accused the trustee of favoritism. Suspicion escalated into lawsuits. Even though the trustee was acting correctly, lack of communication created a powder keg.

2.4 Successor Trustees and Backups

No role in a trust lasts forever. The grantor will pass away. The original trustee may decline to serve, grow ill, or die. That's why naming successor trustees is vital. Think of them as understudies in a play: they may never take the stage, but if the lead cannot perform, they step in seamlessly.

Good Practices for Successors

- Always name more than one backup.
- Choose people or institutions likely to remain available.
- Consider co-trustees carefully: they provide balance but may create friction.

You also have the option of giving beneficiaries the power to select or replace a trustee. This can be a safeguard, allowing the trust to adapt if a chosen trustee proves unfit. The key is flexibility: your trust should not depend on a single person's availability.

Case Study – Well-Prepared Successors

A woman listed three successor trustees in order. When her first choice declined due to health, the second stepped in immediately. The process remained seamless.

Case Study – The Absent Backup

A man named only his brother as successor trustee. When the brother died unexpectedly, the trust had no backup. A court had to intervene, adding delays and costs.

2.5 How the Roles Work Together

When properly arranged, these roles create a simple, self-sustaining structure. You, the grantor, place assets into the trust. The trustee manages them according to your written plan. The beneficiaries receive the benefits in the manner you have chosen. If someone cannot perform their role, a successor steps in.

The Harmony Analogy

Think of the trust as a symphony:

- The grantor writes the score.
- The trustee conducts.
- The beneficiaries listen and enjoy the music.
- Successors wait in the wings, ready to pick up the baton.

When each role functions well, the music flows. When one falters, dissonance creeps in.

2.6 Takeaway

A trust only works if the right players are cast in the right parts. The grantor provides the vision, the trustee executes it, the beneficiaries receive the fruits, and the successors ensure continuity. By understanding these roles, you can avoid missteps, prevent conflict, and give your trust the durability it needs to last. In the next chapter, we will compare trusts with wills and other planning tools to see how each actor's role changes in different legal contexts.

Chapter 3

The Grantor

The grantor—also called the settlor, trustor, or trust maker—is the one who breathes life into a trust. This chapter explores who the grantor is, what powers and responsibilities they hold, how they shape the trust's destiny, and common mistakes to avoid.

3.1 Why the Grantor Matters

Every trust begins with an idea in someone's mind: "I want to protect my family, avoid probate, and leave clear instructions." That person is the grantor. Without the grantor, there is no trust. They decide what property to place inside, what rules to write, and who should benefit. If the trustee is the pilot, the grantor is the engineer who designed the plane.

3.2 Names and Terminology

Different states and lawyers use different words, but they all mean the same thing:

- **Grantor.** The most common American term.
- **Settlor.** Often used in older or more formal documents.
- **Trustor.** Common in western states.
- **Trust Maker.** A plain-English alternative used in consumer-friendly guides.

Do not be confused. Whether called grantor, settlor, or trust maker, this role is the person who initiates the process.

3.3 Core Powers of the Grantor

Creating the Trust

The grantor decides:

- What type of trust to create (revocable, irrevocable, special purpose).
- Which property to transfer.

- Who will serve as trustee and successor trustees.
- Who the beneficiaries are, and under what terms they receive assets.

Funding the Trust

A trust is only as strong as the assets placed inside. The grantor must retitle deeds, change account ownership, and update beneficiary designations. Otherwise, the trust becomes a hollow shell.

Amending or Revoking

In a revocable trust, the grantor can:

- Amend terms as circumstances change.
- Add or remove property.
- Revoke the trust entirely if it no longer serves its purpose.

Irrevocable trusts, by contrast, lock the grantor out once assets are transferred, which can be useful for tax planning or asset protection but requires careful forethought.

3.4 Responsibilities of the Grantor

Being a grantor is not just signing documents. It requires foresight and clarity:

- **Clarity of Intent.** Ambiguity breeds conflict. Vague instructions like "divide fairly" cause disputes.
- **Consistency.** If assets are left out of the trust, probate may still be required.
- **Realism.** The grantor must consider whether their instructions are practical and enforceable.
- **Communication.** Families often fight less when the grantor explains their reasoning in advance.

3.5 The Grantor During Life

While alive and competent, grantors usually continue to control their trust assets directly, especially in revocable living trusts. They may serve as their own trustee, writing checks, buying investments, or selling property as before. In this phase, the trust often feels invisible, but its scaffolding is quietly in place.

3.6 The Grantor at Incapacity

A will is powerless if the grantor becomes incapacitated. A trust, however, shifts authority to the successor trustee without court intervention. The grantor's prior planning ensures their bills are paid and their property is managed even while they cannot act. This is one of the trust's greatest strengths.

3.7 The Grantor at Death

At death, the grantor's role ceases, but their voice continues through the trust document. The rules they wrote guide the trustee, protect beneficiaries, and direct distributions. In this sense, the grantor is like an author whose story continues after they are gone.

3.8 Common Mistakes Grantors Make

Failing to Fund

A beautifully drafted trust that owns nothing accomplishes nothing. Assets must be moved into the trust.

Vagueness

Instructions such as "divide equally" may sound simple but create confusion when assets are illiquid or sentimental.

Over-Complication

Some grantors draft overly rigid rules (e.g., "My children must use their inheritance to buy a home within two years"). Life rarely follows such narrow scripts.

Silence

Grantors who never discuss their trust may leave behind hurt feelings and suspicions. A short conversation during life can prevent years of disputes.

3.9 Case Studies

The Thoughtful Planner

Maria, a widow with two children, created a revocable trust. She transferred her home and savings into it, named her sister as successor trustee, and wrote clear instructions for staged distributions. When she passed, her children avoided probate and received funds responsibly.

The Empty Trust

John signed a trust but never transferred his house or accounts. At death, the trust owned nothing, and his estate went through probate anyway. His effort was wasted because he neglected funding.

The Vague Visionary

A father instructed that his children "divide things fairly." One child wanted to keep the family home; the others wanted it sold. Years of litigation followed, costing more than the property was worth.

3.10 Checklist for Grantors

- Decide on the type of trust and its goals.
- Choose trustees and successors carefully.
- Write clear, specific instructions.
- Transfer assets into the trust promptly.
- Review and update every 3–5 years or after major life events.
- Communicate your intentions with key family members.

3.11 Takeaway

The grantor is the architect and visionary of the trust. Their clarity, foresight, and follow-through determine whether the structure stands strong or collapses into confusion. More than anyone else, the grantor sets the tone: a trust can be a gift of peace and stability, or a seed of conflict. By being thoughtful, precise, and proactive, grantors can ensure their trust endures as a source of guidance and protection for generations.

Chapter 4

Trustees

What a trustee is, how to choose one, what the job requires, how to avoid personal liability, and how beneficiaries stay informed. Practical checklists and model language included.

4.1 Why Trustees Matter

If the grantor is the playwright and the trust is the script, the trustee is the director and stage manager rolled into one. The trustee is the person who makes the trust come alive. Without someone to manage the assets and carry out the instructions, a trust is nothing more than paper. Unlike an executor, whose job usually ends within a year after death, a trustee's role can stretch for decades. Unlike an agent under a power of attorney, whose authority ends at death, a trustee's authority may begin during life and continue long after. That continuity is what makes trustees so important.

4.2 Who Can Serve as Trustee

Choosing the right trustee is one of the most consequential decisions in the entire trust process. A brilliant trust document with a poor trustee is like a beautifully designed car in the hands of an unskilled driver: it may look fine on paper, but the journey will be rocky. Understanding the different categories of trustees, their advantages and drawbacks, and the qualifications that truly matter will help you make a sound choice.

Individual vs. Corporate Trustees

Individual Trustees. Many families instinctively appoint an individual trustee—often a spouse, adult child, sibling, or close friend. The advantages are clear: personal knowledge of family history, shared values, and often lower or no fees. Individual trustees may also have an easier time earning trust from beneficiaries who see them as "one of us."

But these same qualities can create tension. Family

trustees may:

- Show favoritism, even unconsciously.
- Struggle to enforce limits (e.g., denying a sibling's request for money).
- Lack financial or legal expertise, leading to mistakes.

Conflicts can escalate quickly when a trustee is "too close" to the beneficiaries. Even the most loving parent or child may find themselves accused of bias.

Corporate Trustees. Banks, trust companies, and professional fiduciaries bring a different set of strengths. They offer:

- Professional expertise in investments, accounting, and compliance.
- Neutrality—no family drama.
- Continuity—institutions rarely die, move, or retire.

The downside is cost (fees can be significant), less personal knowledge of the family, and sometimes a reputation for rigidity. Corporate trustees work best for long-term trusts, large estates, or situations where neutrality is critical.

Blended Approaches. Some trusts appoint both: a

family member to keep the human touch, and a corporate trustee to handle technical matters. This "team approach" can balance warmth and professionalism—though it may also increase complexity and cost.

Eligibility and Disqualifiers

A trustee must be legally competent and of sound mind. But beyond the law, practical eligibility matters just as much:

- **Financial Stability.** Someone drowning in debt may not be a wise custodian.
- **Organizational Skills.** Trustees must track deadlines, investments, and paperwork.
- **Geography.** An out-of-state trustee may face legal hurdles or logistical delays.
- **Reputation.** Trustees with prior bankruptcies, criminal convictions, or histories of dishonesty raise red flags.

It is better to appoint a "boring but reliable" cousin than a charismatic sibling who cannot balance a checkbook.

Co-Trustees and Directed Trusts

Co-Trustees. Appointing two or more trustees can provide balance and oversight. For example, two siblings may keep each other accountable. But co-trustees must agree, and disagreements can deadlock administration. To prevent paralysis, the trust should specify:

- Whether decisions require unanimity or majority vote.
- Who breaks ties if disagreements persist.

Directed Trusts. Modern law allows "directed trusts," where duties are split. One trustee manages investments, another approves distributions, and sometimes a third—called a trust protector—oversees or resolves disputes. This division spreads responsibility but requires careful drafting to avoid confusion.

4.3 How Trustees Are Replaced

Trusts are designed to endure, but people are not. Trustees may decline, resign, or fail. Understanding how they step in and out is crucial.

Appointment Mechanics

The trust document itself is the "job description." It names the initial trustee and outlines how successors take office. Usually:

- The trustee signs an acceptance document.
- Banks and investment firms require a certification of trust.
- Successors present proof of death, incapacity, or resignation of the prior trustee.

This process avoids court involvement if the trust is drafted properly.

Resignation and Removal

Trustees may resign by giving notice to beneficiaries and co-trustees. They must transfer records and assets promptly. Removal can occur in three ways:

- **By the trust.** Some trusts grant beneficiaries or protectors power to remove a trustee.
- **By agreement.** If all beneficiaries and the trustee agree, resignation is usually smooth.
- **By court.** Courts remove trustees for incapacity, mismanagement, or conflict of interest.

Clear succession rules reduce disruption.

Drafting Levers

Grantors can build flexibility into the document:

- Authorizing a majority of beneficiaries to replace a trustee.
- Naming a neutral "trust protector" with oversight power.
- Allowing resignation without court involvement.

These levers prevent a trust from being trapped with an unwilling or unfit trustee.

4.4 Core Fiduciary Duties

Trustees are fiduciaries, meaning the law holds them to the highest standard of honesty and care. These duties are not optional—they are the backbone of the role.

Duty of Loyalty

The trustee must act solely in the beneficiaries' best interests. They cannot:

- Lend trust money to themselves.
- Buy trust assets for personal use.

- Favor one beneficiary at the expense of another.

Even the appearance of conflict can be damaging.

Duty of Prudence

Trustees must manage assets wisely. This is often called the "prudent investor rule." It does not mean avoiding all risk, but rather:

- Diversifying investments.
- Balancing growth and safety.
- Seeking professional advice when needed.

Duty of Impartiality

Trustees must balance competing interests. For example, income beneficiaries may want high-yield investments, while remainder beneficiaries prefer growth. The trustee must weigh both fairly.

Duty to Inform and Account

Beneficiaries are entitled to know what is happening. Trustees must:

- Provide annual accountings.
- Share key documents on request.

- Notify beneficiaries of important changes.

Silence breeds suspicion. Transparency preserves trust.

Duty to Follow Terms

The trustee must carry out the trust exactly as written. If language is unclear, they must seek clarification rather than improvise. Courts will not excuse trustees who "meant well" but ignored the document.

4.5 Distribution Standards

Distributions are often the most sensitive part of trust administration. Money touches emotions, and beneficiaries often disagree on what is "fair." Clear standards guide trustees, but discretion still requires wisdom.

HEMS Standard

The most common yardstick is Health, Education, Maintenance, and Support (HEMS). Trustees may pay:

- Tuition and educational expenses.
- Medical care, insurance, and therapy.
- Reasonable living expenses such as housing and food.

But they may refuse frivolous requests like sports cars or luxury vacations. The HEMS standard protects trustees by providing an objective rule.

Mandatory vs. Discretionary

Some trusts mandate distributions—e.g., "$10,000 annually" or "one-third of the estate at age 25." Mandatory terms leave little room for judgment but can strain liquidity if assets are tied up.

Discretionary trusts give trustees power to decide when and how much to distribute. This flexibility allows adaptation but requires documentation to prove fairness. Trustees should record:

- The request made.
- The factors considered.
- The decision reached and why.

Special Situations

Special Needs Beneficiaries. Trustees must avoid jeopardizing government benefits. Payments should often be made directly to service providers, not to the beneficiary.

Substance Abuse Concerns. Some trusts require

proof of sobriety before distributions. Trustees may face the uncomfortable role of monitoring or testing beneficiaries.

Spendthrift Clauses. These protect assets from creditors or reckless spending. The trustee becomes a financial gatekeeper, sometimes against the beneficiary's wishes.

Case Studies

- A trustee funded a grandson's college tuition but denied his request for a sports car. By citing the HEMS standard, the trustee avoided conflict and preserved assets.
- In another case, a discretionary trustee gave uneven distributions based on "gut feelings." Siblings sued, alleging favoritism. The lack of documentation hurt the trustee's defense.

The lesson: standards guide, discretion requires care, and documentation protects.

4.6 First 90 Days Checklist

The first three months of serving as trustee are critical. Many of the mistakes trustees make—commingling funds, missing deadlines, losing track of assets—happen in this window. Think of the first 90 days as "orientation." The actions you take here set the tone for the rest of the administration. Slow down, document everything, and resist the temptation to "wing it."

Onboarding

The onboarding phase is about understanding the job before you act. Just as a pilot runs through a pre-flight checklist before leaving the runway, a trustee should complete these steps before making major decisions:

- **Obtain and review the trust document.** Read it carefully, cover to cover. Highlight terms that relate to your powers, duties, and distribution standards. Create a working summary or "trust abstract" for quick reference.

- **Secure professional support.** Consider engaging an estate attorney or CPA to explain confusing provisions. Even a one-hour consult can prevent months of trouble.

- **Apply for a tax ID number (EIN) if needed.** Revocable trusts may use the grantor's Social Security number during life, but after death, the trust typically needs its own EIN.

- **Open dedicated bank and brokerage**

accounts. Never use personal accounts. Commingling funds is a trustee's cardinal sin.

- **Secure deeds, titles, and insurance policies.** Transfer real property into the trust's name if not already done. Notify insurance carriers of the trust ownership to avoid coverage lapses.
- **Create a trustee binder or digital vault.** Collect the trust, account statements, tax returns, contact info, and key correspondence in one organized location.

Inventory and Valuation

You cannot manage what you do not measure. Within the first 90 days:

- **List all assets.** Bank accounts, brokerage accounts, retirement plans, life insurance, real estate, vehicles, business interests, personal property, intellectual property, and digital assets.
- **Collect statements and evidence of ownership.** Print, download, or request official documentation.
- **Order appraisals.** Real estate, jewelry, collectibles, and closely held businesses often

require professional valuations.

- **Note liabilities.** Mortgages, credit cards, medical bills, and tax obligations belong on your balance sheet too.
- **Create an initial net worth snapshot.** This becomes your baseline for accounting and future comparisons.

Think of this as taking inventory before running a store. Without it, you cannot know what you are protecting or what risks you face.

Notifications and Calendaring

Communication and organization prevent most disputes. Within the first three months:

- **Notify beneficiaries.** Send a formal letter of appointment. Include your contact information and a general explanation of their rights.
- **Notify institutions.** Banks, brokers, tenants, insurance companies, and others must know you are the new decision-maker.
- **Set a calendar.** Note tax deadlines (federal and state), appraisal renewals, insurance expirations, and key trust anniversaries. Digital reminders are

invaluable.

- **Document the timeline.** Keep a trustee log noting when notices went out, when you received responses, and any pending obligations.

4.7 Investments and Risk

After stabilization, trustees must shift to ongoing management. Money does not stand still. Investments must be tended, risks managed, and cash kept ready for near-term needs.

Building an Investment Policy

A written Investment Policy Statement (IPS) is the trustee's roadmap. It should outline:

- Objectives (e.g., preserve capital, provide income, support beneficiaries).
- Risk tolerance (how much volatility the trust can endure).
- Asset allocation targets (e.g., 60% stocks, 30% bonds, 10% alternatives).
- Rebalancing rules (e.g., annual, or when an asset class drifts more than 5%).

- Benchmarking (e.g., compare performance to S&P 500 or bond indices).

Without an IPS, investment decisions appear arbitrary and expose the trustee to liability.

Liquidity Planning

Trusts must have cash available for taxes, distributions, and emergencies. Illiquid assets like real estate or private equity can trap wealth. Trustees should:

- Maintain a "cash bucket" of 6–12 months of expected expenses.
- Consider lines of credit as backup.
- Plan sales of illiquid assets early, before crises force "fire sales."

Liquidity is not just about math; it is about sleep. Beneficiaries sleep easier when they know bills and distributions can be met.

Delegation and Oversight

Trustees may hire advisors—investment managers, property managers, CPAs—but must monitor them:

- Review advisor contracts annually.

- Compare performance to benchmarks.
- Keep written notes of meetings and decisions.

Delegation is allowed; abdication is not.

4.8 Taxes and Reporting

What Changes When

During the grantor's life, most revocable trusts are tax-neutral: the grantor reports income on their personal return. After death or conversion to irrevocable status, the trust may need to file its own Form 1041. Trustees must:

- Know when the trust's "tax personality" changes.
- Track fiscal year vs. calendar year elections.
- Work with professionals to avoid penalties.

Information Returns and K-1s

Beneficiaries receiving income must get Schedule K-1s. This requires:

- Collecting data from banks and brokers.
- Coordinating with CPAs early (don't wait until April).

- Delivering K-1s promptly so beneficiaries can file taxes.

Recordkeeping

Good records are a trustee's shield:

- Keep receipts, invoices, and distribution notes.
- Store emails and letters in organized folders.
- Create an annual "Trustee Report" for transparency.

4.9 Compensation & Expenses

Reasonable Compensation

Trustees are entitled to fair pay unless the trust prohibits it. Options include:

- Flat annual fees.
- Hourly rates with time logs.
- Percentage of assets under management (common for corporate trustees).

Transparency avoids resentment.

Reimbursable Expenses

Trustees can be reimbursed for:

- Travel to manage property.
- Postage, notary, and copying costs.
- Professional fees (lawyers, CPAs, appraisers).

They cannot bill the trust for personal expenses or "lost wages" from other jobs unless the trust explicitly allows it.

Indemnity and Insurance

Well-drafted trusts indemnify trustees for good-faith mistakes. Still, trustees may wish to purchase fiduciary liability insurance. This protection is especially important in high-conflict families.

4.10 Communication

Most lawsuits against trustees begin not with theft but with silence. Beneficiaries fear what they cannot see.

Cadence and Format

Best practices include:

- Quarterly letters summarizing assets, income, and decisions.
- Annual accountings with full detail.
- Plain-English explanations alongside technical statements.

Expectation Setting

Trustees should educate beneficiaries about:

- What the trust permits and forbids.
- The process for requesting distributions.
- How long requests typically take to process.

Clarity reduces conflict.

Conflict De-escalation

When disputes arise:

- Document every discussion.
- Use neutral language in correspondence.
- Consider mediation before litigation.

4.11 Problem Spots

Top Pitfalls

- **Commingling funds.** Even temporary mixing of accounts is dangerous.
- **Missed deadlines.** Tax penalties and lapsed insurance can cost dearly.
- **Bias.** Favoring one child undermines legitimacy.
- **Neglect.** Ignoring investments or properties erodes value.

Red Flags in Distributions

Requests that should raise caution include:

- "Emergency" cash requests with no documentation.
- Repeated loans to the same beneficiary.
- Pressure from creditors, spouses, or business partners.

4.12 Advanced Tools

Decanting and Nonjudicial Settlements

In states that allow it, decanting lets trustees pour assets from one trust into another with updated terms. Nonjudicial settlement agreements permit beneficiaries and trustees to resolve issues without court.

Directed and Divided Trusteeships

Splitting duties can make sense:

- An investment trustee manages portfolios.
- A distribution trustee approves spending.

This division spreads risk but requires clear drafting.

4.13 Special Asset Playbook

Real Estate

Trustees managing property should:

- Verify insurance coverage.
- Schedule regular inspections.
- Collect rent and enforce leases.

- Budget for taxes and repairs.

Closely Held Businesses

Business assets require:

- Reviewing buy-sell agreements.
- Monitoring management succession.
- Balancing reinvestment vs. distributions.

Digital Assets and IP

Digital assets are easily overlooked. Trustees should:

- Secure passwords and access credentials.
- Manage websites, domain names, and online accounts.
- Track royalties from intellectual property.

4.14 Case Studies

The Overcommitted Trustee

A daughter agreed to serve as trustee while working full-time and raising children. She quickly fell behind on notices and accounting. Beneficiaries lost confidence, and she eventually resigned. The lesson: willingness is not the same as capacity.

The Sibling Stalemate

Two brothers served as co-trustees. They disagreed on nearly every decision, paralyzing the trust. A neutral professional trustee was eventually appointed, restoring order. The lesson: co-trustees need clear tie-break rules.

The Special Needs Misstep

A trustee gave cash directly to a disabled beneficiary, unintentionally jeopardizing government benefits. Proper structuring—paying providers directly—would have avoided harm. The lesson: special circumstances require special handling.

4.15 Trustee Boundaries

Trustees are often family members pulled into an emotionally heavy role. The weight can be immense. Trustees should:

- **Set boundaries.** Saying "no" is sometimes the most loving act.
- **Seek professional help.** Delegating to lawyers,

accountants, and advisors is not weakness—it is prudence.

- **Step aside when needed.** If the role becomes overwhelming, it is better to resign than to fail.

4.16 Key Takeaways

- The first 90 days are decisive—set systems early.
- Trustees are fiduciaries first, family members second.
- Documentation, diversification, and transparency are the three shields against liability.
- A good trustee preserves not just money but relationships.
- When uncertain, pause, seek advice, and write everything down.

Chapter 5

The Beneficiaries

Beneficiaries are the reason a trust exists. They are the people or organizations who receive the benefit of the grantor's planning. This chapter explores who beneficiaries are, the rights they hold, the expectations they carry, and how trustees manage their needs and demands. It also examines the conflicts that often arise and offers tools to avoid them.

5.1 Who Are Beneficiaries?

A beneficiary is any person or entity named in the trust to receive assets, income, or some benefit. They are the focus of the trust, the "why" behind all the planning. Beneficiaries may be children, grandchildren, spouses, friends, charities, or even pets. The trust document defines who qualifies, when they qualify, and under what circumstances. Without beneficiaries, a trust has no purpose.

Current vs. Remainder Beneficiaries

- **Current beneficiaries** have rights now—such as a surviving spouse entitled to income or distributions during their lifetime.
- **Remainder beneficiaries** receive benefits later, after another beneficiary's interest ends (for example, children inheriting after the spouse's death).

Individual vs. Charitable Beneficiaries

- **Individual beneficiaries** may include family, friends, or specific people the grantor wants to provide for.
- **Charitable beneficiaries** can be churches, schools, hospitals, or nonprofit causes the grantor supports. Charitable trusts often carry special tax treatment.

Contingent Beneficiaries

These are "backup" recipients—people who inherit if the primary beneficiary dies first or disclaims their share. Contingent beneficiaries prevent gaps and ensure assets do not default to probate.

5.2 Rights of Beneficiaries

Beneficiaries are not passive spectators; they have legally recognized rights. These rights vary by state law and by the trust's terms, but they commonly include:

Right to Information

Beneficiaries have the right to know that the trust exists, who the trustee is, and what their interest is. This often includes receiving copies of the trust instrument or at least a summary. Without information, they cannot protect their interests.

Right to Accountings

Trustees must keep records of income, expenses, and distributions. Beneficiaries are entitled to periodic accountings to ensure transparency. This duty exists to prevent misuse or mismanagement. Accountings also allow beneficiaries to spot errors early and request corrections before they snowball.

Right to Distributions

If the trust requires mandatory payments (e.g., "$5,000 per year to each child"), beneficiaries can enforce that right in court. If distributions are discretionary, they have the right to expect the trustee to exercise discretion in good faith. This prevents arbitrary denials or favoritism.

Right to Fair Treatment

Trustees must treat beneficiaries impartially. One cannot be unfairly favored over another unless the trust explicitly permits it. Impartiality does not mean "equal," but rather "fair according to the trust's terms."

Right to Enforce the Trust

Ultimately, beneficiaries have the power to hold trustees accountable in court if duties are breached. They are the check and balance on trustee power.

5.3 Expectations and Realities

Beneficiaries often approach trusts with high expectations. They may imagine immediate access to wealth, or they may feel entitled to more than what the trust provides. Reality can be sobering: distributions may be limited, controlled, or delayed. Trustees may deny requests for funds if they fall outside the trust's terms.

This tension between expectation and reality is one of the most common sources of conflict. For example, a child who believes "Dad wanted me to have the house" may be disappointed to learn that the trust requires the house to be sold and proceeds divided.

Emotional Layer

Inheritances carry symbolic meaning. A grandparent's watch or family home may matter more to a beneficiary than stock shares of equal value. If trusts do not account for sentimental items, disputes often erupt.

Financial Layer

Some beneficiaries view the trust as a safety net; others see it as a windfall. Trustees must manage both attitudes carefully, balancing legitimate needs against long-term sustainability.

5.4 Special Types

Minor Children

Trusts often protect minors by delaying distributions until adulthood or staggered ages (e.g., one-third at 25, one-third at 30, balance at 35). Until then, trustees may use funds for education, medical care, or support. These structures keep a teenager from receiving—and wasting—a fortune overnight.

Beneficiaries With Special Needs

Special needs trusts preserve eligibility for government benefits. Distributions may be made directly to providers (e.g., for housing or therapy) rather than to the beneficiary, preventing disqualification. Without proper structuring, well-meaning gifts can unintentionally cut off essential benefits.

Spendthrift Beneficiaries

Some beneficiaries struggle with money management, face creditor risks, or have unstable lifestyles. A spendthrift clause prevents them from selling or pledging their trust interest and shields the assets from creditors. It places the trustee in the role of gatekeeper to preserve the inheritance.

Charitable Beneficiaries

Charitable trusts must balance donor intent with legal compliance. Charities may monitor trustees closely to ensure distributions are timely and in line with mission. Unlike individuals, charities have institutional structures and often send staff or lawyers to enforce their rights.

5.5 Common Problems

Entitlement and Misunderstanding

Some beneficiaries assume they "own" the trust assets immediately. In reality, legal ownership rests with the trustee, subject to the rules of the trust. This misconception fuels demands that trustees may not lawfully meet.

Family Conflict

Siblings often clash when one serves as trustee and others as beneficiaries. Accusations of favoritism or mismanagement are common. Even if the trustee acts properly, family dynamics may color perceptions.

Impatience

Beneficiaries may push for early distributions, even when the trust requires waiting until a certain age or event. Impatience can cause pressure, resentment, and sometimes lawsuits.

Lack of Communication

When trustees fail to explain decisions, beneficiaries may grow suspicious, assuming wrongdoing even when none exists. Silence erodes trust more quickly than almost anything else.

5.6 Case Studies

The Suspicious Sibling

A sister serving as trustee made correct but poorly explained decisions. Her brothers, left in the dark, accused her of hiding money. Only after producing detailed accountings did the conflict ease. **Lesson: transparency matters.**

The Special Needs Success

A disabled son was cared for through a properly drafted special needs trust. Funds paid for therapy, equipment, and recreation without threatening benefits. **Lesson: tailored planning works.**

The Spender

A young adult who received his inheritance outright at 18 spent it all within two years. His siblings, whose distributions were delayed until 25, used their funds for homes and education. **Lesson: staged distributions protect beneficiaries from themselves.**

The Charity's Watchful Eye

A university named as beneficiary of a trust noticed late payments. Its counsel pressed the trustee, who corrected the schedule. **Lesson: charitable beneficiaries often enforce rights aggressively.**

5.7 Checklist

- Know your status: Are you current, remainder, or contingent?
- Request copies or summaries of the trust if entitled.
- Review annual accountings carefully; ask questions early.
- Understand that "impartial" does not always mean

"equal."

- Manage expectations: a trustee cannot do more than the trust allows.
- Use communication and mediation before litigation.

5.8 Practical Toolkit

Sample Questions to Ask a Trustee

- What is my status (current, remainder, contingent)?
- What standards govern distributions (HEMS, discretionary, mandatory)?
- How often will I receive accountings?
- Who are the other beneficiaries?

Red Flags for Beneficiaries

- Long delays in communication from the trustee.
- Refusal to provide basic information.
- Distributions inconsistent with the trust terms.

5.9 Takeaway

Beneficiaries are the heart of the trust. The grantor creates, the trustee manages, but it is the beneficiaries who ultimately receive the fruits. Understanding their rights, managing expectations, and fostering open communication can transform the trust from a source of conflict into a source of stability.

For beneficiaries themselves, knowledge is power: knowing what they are entitled to, and what they are not, allows them to engage constructively rather than combatively. Trusts succeed when beneficiaries respect the structure, trustees honor their duties, and grantors write clear instructions that reduce ambiguity. In that balance, families find peace and legacies endure.

Chapter 6

Estate Planning

When people first think about estate planning, their minds usually go straight to a will. Wills are familiar. They are the star of countless novels and films, read aloud in dramatic voices: "I hereby bequeath my estate to. . . " The image is iconic. But in real life, a will is only one tool in the estate-planning toolbox. It is a starting point, not a finish line. Trusts, wills, and other planning instruments each play distinct roles. Understanding the differences helps you see why many people make a trust the centerpiece of their plan—and why others use a combination.

This chapter takes a deep dive into wills, trusts, and other estate planning tools. We will trace their history, compare their strengths and weaknesses, and illustrate how each works through real-life examples. By the end, you will not only know the legal mechanics but also see how these tools play out in everyday family life.

6.1 A Starting Point

For centuries, the will has been the cornerstone of estate planning. In fact, the very word "testament" (as in "last will and testament") comes from Latin roots meaning "to bear witness." The idea is simple: at the end of your life, you bear witness to your wishes by writing them down. Courts then enforce them. Wills remain familiar, accessible, and powerful. But like any tool, they have both strengths and serious limitations.

Definition and Core Purpose

At its heart, a will is a written document that directs how your property should be distributed after death. It ensures that your voice continues even when you cannot speak. A valid will must usually meet certain formalities—such as being signed by the testator (the person making the will), witnessed by others, and sometimes notarized, depending on state law.

The will does several important things:

- **Distributes Property.** You can state who receives specific assets—your home, your bank accounts, your personal belongings.
- **Names Guardians.** A will allows parents to nominate guardians for minor children. This is one of the most crucial functions, since a trust cannot handle guardianship.
- **Appoints an Executor.** The executor (sometimes called a "personal representative") is the person who carries out the instructions in the will, pays debts, and manages the probate process.
- **Acts as a Catch-All.** Even if you have a trust, a will can serve as a backup to transfer assets not placed in the trust. Lawyers often call this a "pour-over will."

Without a will, the state decides. Each state has "intestacy laws" that dictate who inherits if you die without instructions. These default rules often create results you would never have chosen. For example, in many states, if you are married with children, your spouse and children split the estate. That may sound fair, but it can force your spouse to sell the house to pay the children their share. A will allows you to avoid such unintended consequences.

Historical Perspective

Wills are ancient. In Roman law, a "testamentum" was a highly formal act, requiring witnesses and rituals. In medieval England, wills were often read aloud in village gatherings to ensure the community enforced them. Today, the requirements are more standardized, but the idea remains the same: a will is your last word. It is still the most widely recognized estate planning document in the United States, even though trusts have grown in popularity.

Limitations of a Will

For all its strengths, a will is not a magic wand. Its limitations are significant:

- **No Effect During Life.** A will is inert until you die. It cannot manage your property if you are in a coma or suffering from dementia. If incapacity strikes, the will is useless.
- **Requires Probate.** To take effect, a will must go through probate court. Probate is the formal legal process of proving the will's validity, identifying assets, paying debts, and distributing what remains. It is slow, public, and often expensive.
- **Public Record.** Probate files are open to anyone.

Your instructions, the value of your estate, and even the squabbles of your heirs become part of the public record.

- **Costs.** Legal fees, court costs, and executor commissions often consume a large share of the estate. Even modest estates can see thousands of dollars vanish in the process.

Thus, while a will is important, it is not sufficient for many families. It is like having only a spare tire for your car—you may get by in an emergency, but you cannot drive smoothly for long without the full set.

Common Myths About Wills

Misunderstandings about wills are everywhere, and they persist because people assume that drafting a single document is the end of estate planning. In truth, a will has serious limitations. Below are some of the most common myths, explained in greater detail:

- **"If I have a will, my family avoids court."** False. A will *requires* probate in nearly every state. The probate process validates the will, oversees payment of debts and taxes, and supervises distribution of property. Even a simple, uncontested will must pass through the probate court, which means delays, costs, and public filings. People are often surprised to learn that a will is essentially a "ticket into court," not a bypass around it.

- **"A will prevents fights."** Not always. While a will can provide clarity, it is often the very document at the center of family disputes. Wills are vulnerable to contests alleging undue influence, fraud, or lack of capacity. The more money, property, or emotion involved, the greater the chance that someone will feel shortchanged and challenge the document. In practice, wills are among the most litigated estate planning instruments.

- **"I don't need a will if I don't have much."** False. Even small estates can cause confusion. Who receives the car? What about family heirlooms, pets, or modest savings accounts? Without a will, state intestacy laws dictate distribution, often in ways that do not reflect personal wishes. A simple, inexpensive will can prevent family members from scrambling or arguing over even modest estates.

- **"My spouse automatically inherits everything."** Not necessarily. State intestacy statutes divide property in different ways. In many jurisdictions, if the deceased is survived by both a spouse and children, the estate is split between them rather than passing entirely to the spouse. This can surprise families and leave a surviving spouse financially vulnerable. A will allows you to control these outcomes rather than rely on statutory defaults.

- **"Wills are private documents."** Incorrect. Once admitted to probate, a will becomes part of the public record. Anyone can review it at the courthouse, which means your financial affairs, family details, and distribution plan are not confidential. For those seeking privacy, a trust is often a better tool.
- **"A will covers all of my assets."** Not always. Certain assets, like retirement accounts, life insurance, and jointly held property, typically pass by beneficiary designation or survivorship and are not controlled by a will. Assuming "everything" is covered by a will leads to overlooked assets and inconsistencies.

Case Example – The Simple Will

A young couple with two children took the responsible step of drafting wills. They named each other as primary beneficiaries and appointed guardians for their children. When the husband died suddenly in a car accident, the will worked as intended: his wife inherited the estate, and because she survived, the guardianship provisions became irrelevant. In this narrow scenario, the will provided clarity and a smooth transition.

But the couple's planning was incomplete. Had both parents died together in the accident, the will's guardianship provisions would have gone into effect. Even so, the court would still have needed to oversee the guardianship process, and competing relatives might have contested custody. Furthermore, probate would have been required to validate and execute the wills, adding expense and delay. This shows that while wills can be effective, they remain limited. They work best as one piece of a larger estate plan rather than a stand-alone solution.

Case Example – The Will Alone

A widowed father left a will dividing his estate equally among his three children. On paper, this seemed simple and fair. But because his home and accounts were not placed in a trust, probate became unavoidable. The process stretched over two years, costing nearly $20,000 in court and attorney's fees. Even worse, tensions grew among the siblings. One child accused another of mismanaging estate funds, and old family wounds resurfaced in bitter arguments. The financial drain was matched by an emotional one.

The father had assumed that a valid will would shield his children from complications. He was wrong. While the will did provide clarity about his intentions, it could not bypass the court system. A living trust or better planning might have preserved not only money but also family relationships.

Case Example – The Lost Will

A woman carefully drafted a will, but she failed to tell her family where the document was kept. After her death, the family searched but could not locate the original. Because the original could not be produced, the court presumed she had revoked it and treated her as having died intestate—without a will. The result was devastating: her assets were divided according to state intestacy law. Her estranged brother, whom she had intentionally excluded, received half her estate, while her closest friends, whom she intended to benefit, received nothing.

This case highlights two important lessons: First, drafting a will is not enough; accessibility and safekeeping matter. Second, probate courts rely heavily on technical rules. If the original document cannot be found, intentions may be disregarded. Storing wills securely but accessibly—and letting trusted people know their location—is essential.

Case Example – The Contested Will

An elderly man revised his will late in life, leaving nearly everything to a new girlfriend. His children were stunned and outraged. They challenged the will in court, arguing that their father lacked mental capacity and was subject to undue influence. The probate litigation lasted nearly four years, consuming the estate with legal fees and souring family relationships permanently. By the time the case ended, very little remained for anyone.

This example underscores a critical truth: even formally valid wills are not immune to challenge. If suspicious circumstances surround their execution—particularly late-life changes benefiting outsiders—they are highly vulnerable. While wills can provide clarity, they cannot guarantee peace. Families fractured by contested wills often suffer financial and emotional costs that dwarf the original inheritance.

Checklist: What a Will Can and Cannot Do

Wills are powerful, but only within their proper boundaries. Understanding what they can and cannot accomplish is essential:

A Will CAN:

- Direct who inherits your property at death, avoiding default intestacy rules.
- Appoint guardians for minor children, giving courts strong guidance about your wishes.
- Name an executor (sometimes called a personal representative) to manage estate administration.
- Serve as a backup to a living trust through a "pour-over" provision, ensuring stray assets still flow into the trust.
- Provide clarity about final wishes, such as funeral or memorial arrangements.
- Serve as a relatively inexpensive entry-level planning tool for people with simple estates.

A Will CANNOT:

- Avoid probate—the court process is required to

validate and execute it.

- Control what happens to your property during your lifetime or if you become incapacitated.
- Keep your estate private—once probated, wills are public record.
- Protect assets from creditors, lawsuits, or spendthrift heirs.
- Override beneficiary designations or survivorship provisions on joint accounts and retirement plans.
- Prevent contests—any interested party may challenge a will's validity in court.

In short, a will is an important but limited tool. It works best in tandem with other planning devices, such as trusts, beneficiary designations, and powers of attorney. Alone, it may provide clarity, but it rarely provides efficiency or privacy.

Practical Guidance

If you have children, you need a will—at least for the guardianship provisions. If you own property, a will provides a baseline of clarity. But a will alone is rarely enough. It should be paired with other tools: a trust for probate avoidance, a power of attorney for incapacity, and advance directives for healthcare decisions. The will is your foundation. The other tools are the walls, roof, and windows. Together they build a house strong enough to shelter your family.

Takeaway

The will remains a starting point for nearly every estate plan. It is simple, familiar, and essential for naming guardians and directing property. But it is only the beginning. Think of it as the opening act, not the whole play. Without supporting instruments, it leaves gaps that courts must fill. With them, it serves as a valuable piece of a complete and resilient estate plan.

6.2 A Living Document

Trusts are often called "the quiet giants" of estate planning. They lack the Hollywood glamour of wills read aloud in wood-paneled courtrooms, but in practice, trusts are the instrument that carry families smoothly through the messiest parts of life and death. Where wills speak only once, trusts speak constantly. They operate during your lifetime, adapt to incapacity, and continue after death. They are truly living documents, evolving with you as long as you take care of them.

Definition and Operation

At its core, a trust is an arrangement: one person (the grantor) transfers property to a manager (the trustee) for the benefit of others (the beneficiaries). The grantor writes the rules in the trust document, and the trustee is legally bound to follow them.

In a revocable living trust, you typically wear two hats: grantor and trustee. You still control your property, pay your bills, and make investments. Nothing feels different in your daily life—until incapacity or death. At that point, your successor trustee steps in seamlessly, without waiting for a judge.

This continuity is the secret strength of trusts. Where wills pause at incapacity and wait for death, trusts bridge the gap.

Historical Roots

The idea of trusts is not new. Medieval crusaders leaving for long campaigns entrusted land to friends to manage for their wives and children. Courts gradually recognized these "uses" as enforceable arrangements, evolving into modern trusts. Over centuries, they spread to common-law countries worldwide.

Even today, different nations view trusts differently:

- In the U.S. and U.K., trusts are central estate planning tools.
- In many civil law countries, trusts are limited or replaced by similar instruments.
- Offshore jurisdictions (like the Cayman Islands) have developed specialized trusts for global wealth management.

The universal appeal is clear: trusts solve the timeless problem of continuity when owners cannot act.

Advantages of Trusts: A Deep Dive

The advantages of trusts are layered and multifaceted. Beyond the basics of privacy and probate avoidance, trusts offer nuanced benefits:

- **Privacy.** Probate records are public; trusts remain private. For families with sensitive situations—second marriages, unequal inheritances, or charitable gifts—privacy shields both dignity and safety.
- **Control.** A will distributes everything at once. A trust lets you shape distributions: lump sums, installments, conditional gifts, or ongoing funds. You can support a child's education while

protecting assets from waste.

- **Continuity.** Incapacity is increasingly common with aging populations. A trust ensures bills get paid and property managed without guardianship proceedings.
- **Efficiency.** Trust transfers happen quickly, often in weeks, while probate can drag for years.
- **Customization.** Special clauses can protect spendthrift heirs, provide for pets, or direct charitable giving for decades.
- **Conflict Reduction.** By reducing court involvement, trusts minimize disputes—though they cannot eliminate family drama entirely.

Expanded Case Studies

The Teacher's Trust. A retired teacher created a trust naming her daughter successor trustee. When dementia set in, her daughter stepped in seamlessly. After death, assets transferred without court. The trust worked exactly as intended.

The Empty Binder. A businessman drafted a trust but never funded it. His assets stayed in his own name. Probate was required, wasting time and money. Lesson:

a trust unfunded is a trust undone.

The Protective Shield. A surgeon, wary of malpractice claims, placed assets in an irrevocable trust for his children. Years later, when sued, those assets were untouchable. The trust shielded the family's future.

The Blended Family. A man with children from a prior marriage used a trust to balance competing interests. His wife could live in the marital home for life, but the property would later pass to his children. Without the trust, conflict was inevitable; with it, peace prevailed.

The Philanthropist. A wealthy donor established a charitable remainder trust, receiving income for life while leaving the remainder to a university. She enjoyed tax advantages and lived to see her philanthropy take shape.

Myths and Misconceptions

Trusts attract myths. Let's tackle the big ones:

- **"Trusts are only for millionaires."** Wrong. Even modest estates benefit by avoiding probate, which consumes proportionally more of small estates.
- **"Trusts avoid all taxes."** Incorrect. Revocable

trusts are tax-neutral during life. Only specialized irrevocable trusts may reduce estate or income taxes.

- **"Signing is enough."** False. Funding—retitling assets—is essential. Without it, probate still applies.
- **"Trusts prevent all fights."** They reduce disputes but cannot cure deep family tensions.

Practical Guidance

To establish a trust effectively, follow these steps:

1. **Clarify Goals.** Do you want to avoid probate, protect children, or reduce taxes?
2. **Select Type.** Revocable living trust for flexibility; irrevocable trust for asset protection or tax planning.
3. **Draft Clearly.** Use professional help when family or finances are complex.
4. **Fund Completely.** Transfer deeds, retitle accounts, update designations.
5. **Inform Key People.** Trustees must know their roles and how to access documents.

6. **Review Regularly.** Revisit every 3–5 years or after major life changes.

Global Comparisons and Cultural Use

Trusts also reflect cultural values:

- In Asia, family trusts often ensure multi-generational continuity of businesses.
- In the Middle East, Islamic law interacts with trust-like structures called waqf.
- In Latin America, fiduciary contracts serve similar functions.

The universality of the idea shows its adaptability: wherever property exists, people need ways to protect and pass it on.

Checklist: Trust Advantages in Plain English

- Keeps family matters private.
- Lets you stay in control while alive.
- Smooths transitions during illness.
- Speeds up inheritance after death.

- Protects vulnerable heirs.
- Allows creative, conditional planning.

Takeaway

A trust is more than paper. It is a living promise—a way of saying, "I will keep caring for my loved ones, even when I cannot." Unlike wills, which wake only after death, trusts walk alongside you in life, illness, and beyond. They require diligence—drafting, funding, and maintenance—but repay that effort with privacy, control, and continuity. When carefully used, a trust is not just a legal tool but a gift of stability, sparing your family the chaos of courts and conflict.

In the orchestra of estate planning, the will may play a single song at the end. The trust conducts the entire performance, ensuring harmony from the first note of incapacity to the final chord of inheritance.

6.3 Other Planning Tools

Trusts and wills do much, but they are not the whole story. Several other tools play supporting roles.

Powers of Attorney

A power of attorney authorizes someone to act for you in financial or healthcare matters while you are alive. Without one, family members may need to seek guardianship through court, a slow and expensive process. Powers of attorney can expire at death, but while alive, they complement a trust.

Advance Directives

Sometimes called "living wills," these documents state your medical treatment preferences if you cannot speak for yourself. They guide doctors and spare your family agonizing decisions. A trust cannot handle healthcare decisions; an advance directive does.

Joint Ownership

Many people place assets in joint tenancy with a spouse or child. This can avoid probate for that asset, as ownership transfers automatically to the survivor. But joint ownership carries risks. If the co-owner has debts, creditors may seize the asset. If relationships sour, disputes arise. Joint ownership is a blunt tool—simple but dangerous if misused.

Beneficiary Designations

Retirement accounts, pensions, and life insurance allow you to name beneficiaries directly. These designations override wills. If your will leaves an account to your daughter but your beneficiary designation lists your ex-spouse, the ex-spouse wins. That is why reviewing beneficiary forms is critical.

6.4 Why Trusts?

So why do many people make trusts the centerpiece? Because trusts combine the best features of other tools:

- They avoid probate like joint ownership—but without co-owner risks.
- They provide ongoing instructions like a power of attorney—but with greater durability.
- They distribute inheritance like a will—but with more flexibility.

In practice, most complete estate plans include both a trust and a will. The trust does the heavy lifting, managing assets during life and after death. The will acts as a "catch-all," covering anything accidentally left outside the trust and naming guardians for minors. Powers of attorney and advance directives provide additional coverage. Used together, these tools create a safety net.

Case Example – The Complete Plan

A couple in California created a living trust, wills, healthcare directives, and powers of attorney. When the husband became incapacitated, his wife managed assets through the trust. When they later passed away, their estate transferred smoothly. Probate was avoided. Guardianship for minor children had been named in the will. Their plan functioned like a well-oiled machine.

6.5 Checklist

- **Will:** Covers property at death, names guardians, but requires probate.
- **Trust:** Manages property during life and after death, avoids probate, provides privacy and control.
- **Power of Attorney:** Authorizes someone to act for you while alive, ends at death.
- **Advance Directive:** Guides healthcare decisions when you cannot.
- **Joint Ownership:** Passes property outside probate, but exposes it to co-owner risks.

- **Beneficiary Designations:** Override wills, must be reviewed regularly.

6.6 Takeaway

Estate planning is not about choosing one tool. It is about combining tools into a cohesive plan. A will provides guardianship and backup. A trust ensures privacy, efficiency, and control. Powers of attorney and advance directives handle incapacity. Joint ownership and beneficiary designations play niche roles. Used wisely, these instruments weave together into a safety net for your family. Used poorly, they create contradictions and confusion. The goal is harmony, not patchwork. That is why many people, after learning the differences, make a living trust the core of their estate plan and use the other tools as supporting players.

Chapter 7

Living Trust

Now that you understand why trusts matter and what types exist, it is time to roll up your sleeves. Setting up a living trust is the moment where planning leaves the realm of ideas and becomes action. It is where you stop talking about "someday" and create a structure that will actually guide your family when you are gone. Many people fear this stage, thinking it requires advanced legal training or years of paperwork. In truth, the process is structured, methodical, and achievable for anyone willing to work step by step.

Think of creating a trust as building a house. You must start with a foundation (deciding on the basics), frame the structure (drafting the document), fill it with furniture and essentials (funding the trust), and finally lock it securely and tell others where the keys are (storing and sharing). Skip any stage, and the house may collapse or sit unused. Complete each stage thoughtfully, and you will have a home that shelters your loved ones for decades to come.

7.1 Step One: Decide

The basics are the foundation. Without a clear foundation, the trust cannot stand. This step is about identifying the key players and the rules of the game.

Defining the Roles

Three roles define every trust:

- **Grantor (You).** The person who creates the trust and sets the rules.
- **Trustee.** The person or institution who manages the trust property.
- **Beneficiaries.** The people or organizations who benefit from the trust.

Choosing a Successor Trustee

The choice of successor trustee is often the most important decision you will make. Consider:

- Location: Can they manage property in your state?
- Skill: Are they organized and financially responsible?
- Neutrality: Will they be fair among siblings or stepchildren?
- Willingness: Do they actually want the job?

Case Study – Good Choice: A woman in Ohio chose her daughter, a CPA, as successor trustee. When she passed away, the daughter handled taxes, paid bills, and distributed funds smoothly. The family praised her competence. **Case Study – Bad Choice:** A man in Florida chose his eldest son, who was deep in debt. The son mismanaged the trust and borrowed funds. The other children sued. The trust became a battlefield.

Clarifying Beneficiaries

Beneficiaries must be identified clearly and precisely. Spell out names, percentages, or conditions. If you want grandchildren to receive funds at age 25, state that explicitly. If you want charitable donations, list the charities by full legal name.

Checklist for Step One:

- Decide whether you will serve as trustee during your life.
- Choose at least two successor trustees (primary and backup).
- Write a clear list of beneficiaries with identifying details.
- Decide how distributions will occur: outright, staggered, conditional, or ongoing.

7.2 Step Two: Draft

Drafting is the framing stage: you are building the structure where everything will live.

DIY or Professional?

The choice between DIY and hiring a lawyer depends on complexity:

- Simple family, modest assets: DIY or online template may work.
- Blended family, high-value estate, business ownership, or special needs: hire a lawyer.

Key Components of a Trust Document

Every trust should include:

- A declaration of creation.
- Appointment of trustee(s).
- Powers and limitations of trustees.
- Beneficiary list and distribution instructions.
- Provisions for incapacity.
- A residuary clause to cover everything else.

State Law Differences

Trust law is state-specific. A California trust may require notarization; a Florida trust may require witnesses. Some states impose duties on trustees that others do not. Always confirm local requirements.

The Value of Clarity

Vagueness invites disaster. Instead of writing "my grandchildren inherit for education," specify whether education includes graduate school, trade school, or study abroad. The more you clarify now, the fewer conflicts later.

Sidebar – Language Matters: Courts have overturned trusts that used ambiguous words like "children" without clarifying whether adopted children were included. Precision protects your intent.

7.3 Step Three: Fund

Funding is furnishing the house. Without furniture, the house looks nice but no one can live in it. A trust without assets is the same: impressive on paper but useless in practice.

How to Fund

Funding means transferring legal ownership into the trust:

- Real estate: record a new deed in the trust's name.
- Bank accounts: retitle to "Your Name, Trustee of Your Trust."
- Investments: work with brokerages to transfer accounts.
- Life insurance/retirement: update beneficiary designations.
- Personal property: use a simple assignment form.

The Ongoing Nature of Funding

Funding is never "done." Every time you buy property, open an account, or change investments, you must check whether it is properly titled.

Case Study – Success: A couple in Colorado kept a running "trust asset list." Every new account was added, every property retitled. When they passed, their children inherited everything smoothly without probate. **Case Study – Failure:** A man in Texas funded his trust in 2000 but forgot to place a vacation home he bought in 2010. That home went through probate, delaying distribution and costing $15,000 in legal fees.

7.4 Step Four: Store

Once your trust is drafted and funded, you must secure and share it.

Where to Store

Options include:

- A fireproof safe at home.
- A safe-deposit box at a bank.
- Your attorney's office (if they agree to store

originals).

Keep digital scans as backups, but remember: some banks and title companies require originals.

Informing Trustees

Tell your successor trustees:

- Where the trust is stored.
- Who your attorney and financial advisors are.
- What their main duties will be.

Letter of Intent

A personal letter can explain your values, reasoning, and hopes. For example, you might explain why one child inherits more than another, or encourage beneficiaries to use funds for education or entrepreneurship. While not legally binding, such letters guide trustees and reduce resentment.

7.5 Common Pitfalls

Here are the pitfalls that sink most trusts:

- **Forgetting to fund.** An unfunded trust is worthless.

- **Wrong trustee choice.** Pick competence, not sentiment.
- **Neglecting updates.** Life events demand revisions.
- **Assuming one size fits all.** Always confirm state compliance.
- **Failing to communicate.** Silence breeds suspicion.
- **Not considering digital assets.** Email, cloud storage, crypto—all need planning.

7.6 Step Five: Maintain

A trust is not static—it grows with your life. Maintenance includes:

- Reviewing every 3–5 years.
- Updating after major life events.
- Keeping your asset list current.
- Checking state law changes.

Example: A couple created a trust in 1990 but never updated it. By 2020, half the assets had been sold, two beneficiaries had died, and new grandchildren were not included. The outdated trust caused confusion and litigation. Regular reviews would have prevented the problem.

7.7 Takeaway

Setting up a living trust is not mystical or overwhelming—it is methodical. Treat it like building and maintaining a house: lay the foundation, build the frame, fill it with essentials, secure it, and keep it updated. The difference between success and failure lies not in complexity but in follow-through. Done right, your trust becomes the backbone of your estate plan, protecting your family and ensuring your intentions are honored. Done wrong, it becomes a binder of wasted effort. The choice is in your hands.

Chapter 8

Uses of Trusts

A trust is not an abstract legal trick—it is a practical tool that addresses the real challenges families face every day. Think of it less as a "document" and more as a Swiss army knife for life planning. It helps you avoid unnecessary court involvement, smooths transitions during illness, balances the interests of different family members, and ensures your children and grandchildren are cared for with foresight. In this chapter, we explore four of the most common, and most human, ways trusts are used.

8.1 Probate Avoidance

Probate sounds harmless enough—it's simply the court process of settling an estate. But ask anyone who has been through it, and they will tell you it is often slow, frustrating, and expensive. Probate can take months or even years, especially if there are disputes or unclear instructions. Court filing fees, attorney's fees, and delays can drain both money and patience. Worse, it all happens in public view: probate records are open to anyone who cares to look.

A trust sidesteps this entire ordeal. Because the trust, not you personally, owns the assets, there is nothing for the court to supervise when you die. The trustee simply distributes the property according to your instructions. For example, instead of your heirs waiting a year to sell your home while the court signs off on paperwork, your trustee can list the house for sale immediately. Instead of bank accounts being frozen until probate is finished, they remain accessible to the trustee. In practice, this can mean the difference between a grieving family smoothly carrying on and a family stuck in red tape while bills pile up.

Consider the story of two neighbors. One died with only a will. His adult children spent nearly eighteen months in probate, paying lawyers and arguing over court procedures. The other had a modest living trust. Her children avoided probate entirely, sold her house within three months, and used the proceeds to cover funeral costs and distribute the rest exactly as she had planned. Both families lived in similar homes with similar assets. The difference was the container she chose.

8.2 Protecting Children

Children may be wonderful, but they are rarely ready to inherit large sums of money at age eighteen. A will without a trust says, "Give everything to my kids outright." That means a teenager could walk away with hundreds of thousands of dollars—money that may vanish as quickly as it arrived. Trusts prevent this by structuring how and when children or grandchildren receive property.

For example, you could create a trust that pays for education and medical needs while your children are under twenty-five, but delays direct access to the inheritance until later. You might decide that at age twenty-five, they receive a portion, at thirty they receive another portion, and at thirty-five they receive the balance. This spacing allows them time to mature, make mistakes on smaller amounts, and develop financial sense before receiving more. Grandparents often use trusts to set aside money for grandchildren's college tuition, ensuring the funds cannot be spent elsewhere.

Trusts also protect vulnerable heirs. Imagine you have a child with special needs who receives government benefits. A direct inheritance could disqualify them from those benefits. A properly drafted trust can provide for their comfort and extras without jeopardizing essential aid. Similarly, a "spendthrift" provision can protect a young adult from creditors, divorce, or even their own reckless spending.

8.3 Blended Families

Modern families are rarely simple. Second marriages, stepchildren, and complicated relationships make estate planning sensitive. Without a trust, conflict is almost guaranteed. A surviving spouse may inherit everything, leaving children from a prior marriage with nothing. Or siblings may fight over what "mom really wanted." A trust allows you to balance these competing interests with clarity.

For example, you can create a trust that provides income and housing for your current spouse during their lifetime, but ensures that after their death, the remaining assets go to your children from your first marriage. This honors both sets of relationships without forcing your family into courtroom battles. Trusts can also prevent manipulation—ensuring that no one can pressure an elderly surviving spouse into rewriting everything after you are gone.

Think of a blended family trust as a peace treaty. It may not erase tensions, but it creates a roadmap that is hard to challenge, reducing the chance of long, costly lawsuits between step-siblings and widows.

8.4 Planning for Incapacity

Death is not the only event that requires planning. Illness, injury, or dementia can leave you unable to manage your affairs for months or years. Without a trust, your family may have to go to court to establish guardianship or conservatorship—a process that is slow, public, and often humiliating. Courts may even appoint a stranger if no family member petitions in time.

A trust avoids this by allowing your successor trustee to step in immediately if you cannot act. They can pay bills, maintain property, and care for dependents, all without court oversight. For example, if you suffer a stroke, your successor trustee can access accounts to keep the mortgage current and arrange in-home care. Without a trust, those same accounts might be frozen until a judge approves access, leaving your family scrambling.

This continuity is priceless. It turns what could be a crisis into a manageable transition. It also spares your loved ones from having to make painful, rushed decisions under stress. By planning for incapacity, you give them stability when they need it most.

8.5 Takeaway

Trusts are not ivory-tower legal creations. They are practical tools that address the ordinary realities of family life: the headaches of probate, the challenges of raising children, the tensions of blended families, and the uncertainty of illness. Each of these situations is common. Each of them can be made easier, calmer, and more predictable with a trust. That is why trusts are not just for "someday." They are for the everyday.

Chapter 9

Taxes and Trusts

Few topics make people more anxious than taxes. Many assume that setting up a trust is a magic way to avoid paying them. The truth is more nuanced. A trust can change the timing and manner of taxation, and in some cases can save money—but often it does not. To understand how taxes intersect with trusts, we need to look at the basic categories: income tax, estate tax, gift tax, and a handful of related concepts (basis, portability, state-level rules, and special elections). The aim of this chapter is to make the landscape clear enough that you can spot what matters in your situation, and know when to bring in a professional.

9.1 Key Concepts

- **Trusts don't automatically reduce tax.** A revocable living trust is usually tax-neutral during your life. Its main advantage is probate avoidance and continuity, not tax savings.
- **Some irrevocable trusts can reduce transfer taxes.** Asset-protection or tax-driven irrevocable trusts can remove assets from your taxable estate, but they come with tradeoffs (control, access, administration).
- **Who pays income tax depends on the trust's status.** "Grantor" vs. "non-grantor" and whether income is distributed or retained are pivotal.
- **State rules vary.** A few states impose estate or inheritance taxes with thresholds far lower than federal levels; some states tax trusts based on where the trustee or grantor lives or where the trust is administered.

9.2 What Changes

During Life (Grantor Phase)

For most families, the primary tool is a revocable living trust. With this type of trust, nothing changes in your tax life while you are alive and competent. You still use your Social Security number, file the same tax returns, and pay taxes just as before. The trust's income and deductions flow straight onto your personal return. There is no separate taxpayer identification number and no additional federal income tax filing for the trust while it remains fully revocable and owned by you for tax purposes.

This surprises people who expect tax savings as the main benefit. In reality, the core benefits of a revocable trust are *probate avoidance*, *privacy*, and *incapacity planning*. Tax savings, if any, come from other structures and strategies layered around or beyond the revocable trust.

After Death (Irrevocable Phase)

At your death, your revocable trust typically becomes irrevocable, and the tax treatment shifts. The trust may need its own taxpayer identification number (EIN), and income earned by the trust after death may be taxed at trust rates rather than your individual rates. The trustee must now pay closer attention to:

- Whether to adopt a calendar or fiscal year for the trust's income tax year.
- Whether distributions made to beneficiaries should "carry out" income to them (reducing trust-level tax).
- Timely filings (fiduciary income tax return, information statements to beneficiaries).

Grantor vs. Non-Grantor Irrevocable Trusts

Not all irrevocable trusts are taxed the same. Some irrevocable trusts are intentionally drafted as *grantor trusts* for income tax purposes, meaning the grantor still pays the tax on trust income even though the assets may be outside the grantor's estate for transfer-tax purposes. Others are *non-grantor trusts* and pay their own tax on retained income. The choice affects who pays the tax bill and can be used strategically.

9.3 Taxes

Federal Estate Tax Basics

The federal estate tax exempts a very large amount of wealth; only a small fraction of estates pay it in any given year. The exemption amount and top rate are set by federal law and can change. A trust alone does not erase estate tax, but certain irrevocable trusts can reduce it by moving appreciation outside your taxable estate or by using exemptions more effectively.

Portability Between Spouses

Federal law permits a surviving spouse to *port* a deceased spouse's unused estate tax exemption, but only if an estate tax return is properly filed for the first spouse. Trust plans for married couples should account for whether portability will be elected and how trust funding (e.g., marital vs. bypass shares) coordinates with that decision.

State Estate and Inheritance Taxes

Several states impose their own estate or inheritance taxes with thresholds far lower than the federal exemption. A family fully exempt at the federal level can still face significant state tax. Because state regimes vary (and change), trust situs (where the trust is administered), the trustee's location, and beneficiary locations can matter.

Generation-Skipping Transfer (GST) Tax

Transfers to "skip persons" (e.g., grandchildren) or to long-lived trusts can implicate GST tax. Many long-term or "dynasty" trusts are designed to allocate GST exemption so that trust assets can benefit multiple generations with reduced transfer-tax friction.

9.4 Lifetime Transfers

The Annual Exclusion and the Lifetime Exemption

Gifts you make during life can be sheltered by the annual exclusion (indexed for inflation) and by your lifetime unified credit, which is shared with the estate tax system. Large gifts may require filing an informational gift tax return even when no tax is due. Married couples can often elect to "split" gifts on a return.

Structuring Gifts Through Trusts

Trusts can stage or aim gifts:

- **Crummey powers** may allow beneficiaries to withdraw limited contributions for a short window, preserving annual-exclusion treatment for gifts to a trust.
- **Education/medical payments** made directly to providers can fall outside gift tax altogether.
- **529 plan front-loading** rules allow multiple years of annual exclusion to be "spread" over time for reporting purposes.

These techniques are common in larger plans but must be implemented precisely.

9.5 Income Taxes

Who Pays and at What Rate

Irrevocable non-grantor trusts are separate taxpayers. They obtain an EIN and file fiduciary income tax returns. Critically, trust tax brackets are *compressed*—trusts reach the highest federal bracket at a very low level of retained income compared with individuals. That makes it essential to decide whether to *retain* income (taxed at the trust) or *distribute* income (taxed to beneficiaries).

Distributable Net Income (DNI) and the 65-Day Election

DNI is the cap on how much income tax character a trust can pass out to beneficiaries in a year. Distributions up to DNI generally shift taxation to beneficiaries via Schedules K-1. Many trusts can also use the so-called *65-day election* (if eligible) to treat certain distributions made in the first 65 days of the following year as if made in the prior year—useful for year-end tax tuning.

The Net Investment Income Tax (NIIT)

Trusts can be subject to the additional tax on net investment income once income exceeds a relatively low threshold for trusts. Coordinating distributions and investment strategy can help manage exposure.

Grantor-Trust "Tax Burn"

Some irrevocable trusts are designed so the grantor pays the trust's income tax bill (while trust assets are outside the grantor's estate). This effectively allows additional wealth transfer because paying the tax reduces the grantor's estate without additional gift reporting.

Drafting must be precise, and reimbursement provisions (if any) require careful thought.

Retirement Accounts and Trusts (High Level)

Retirement accounts have special rules. For most non-spouse beneficiaries, federal law requires payout within a defined period. Certain trust structures ("see-through" trusts) may be needed to preserve intended timelines. Because the rules are technical and evolving, coordinate beneficiary designations and trust terms carefully.

S Corporation Stock

Trusts holding S corporation shares must qualify under special regimes (e.g., QSST or ESBT). Each path has distinct income tax consequences and eligibility requirements. This is specialized—get advice before naming a trust as an S-corp shareholder.

9.6 Basis at Death

Assets included in a decedent's taxable estate typically receive a basis adjustment to fair market value at death (up or down). This "step-up" can reduce capital gains on later sale. Assets outside the estate (e.g., in certain completed-gift irrevocable trusts) may *not* receive that adjustment. Balancing estate-tax reduction against basis planning is part of optimizing overall results.

9.7 Help?

You likely need a tax professional when any of the following are true:

- Multiple real properties in different states, or a change of domicile/situs.
- A closely held business, private equity, or S-corp shares.
- Substantial retirement accounts with trust beneficiaries.
- Gifting programs using trusts, Crummey powers, or GST allocation.
- Anticipated taxable estate or state-level estate/inheritance tax exposure.
- Cross-border assets or beneficiaries.

Accountants, financial advisors, and estate attorneys can coordinate elections, filings, and drafting so your trust does more than just avoid probate.

9.8 Takeaway

Trusts are not tax magic. They are about control, privacy, and efficiency first. Tax planning is a powerful bonus that matters mainly for larger or more complex estates. If your estate is modest, focus on funding the trust and keeping it current. If your estate is significant—or your assets are specialized—use the trust as a base and bring in professionals to build the tax strategy around it.

Chapter 10

Common Mistakes

Creating a trust is a powerful step, but it is only half the battle. A trust is not a "set it and forget it" project. It is a living structure that needs to be properly built, furnished, and maintained. Many families mistakenly believe that signing the trust document is the end of the journey. In reality, it is just the beginning. Without careful follow-through, the best-written trust can fail, leaving heirs with the very mess you intended to avoid.

This chapter explores the most common mistakes people make when setting up and maintaining trusts. These errors are not rare—they are widespread. Courts across the country are filled with cases that could have been avoided with more attention. Fortunately, each mistake is preventable if you know what to watch for. Treat this chapter as your "caution board."

10.1 Forgetting to Fund

The number one mistake, by a wide margin, is failing to fund the trust. "Funding" means transferring ownership of your assets into the trust or aligning beneficiary designations with the trust. Without it, your trust is like a safe bolted to the floor but left empty.

How it happens: Someone pays for a beautifully drafted trust, then never retitles the deed, never changes account ownership, never updates life insurance or retirement plan beneficiaries. Years later, the family discovers that the trust owns nothing. Probate follows.

Case in point: A widow spent thousands on a trust but left her house and primary bank account outside it. Her children still had to open a probate case to sell the property. Money and time were lost, and siblings disagreed on sale terms. The trust sat in a drawer—legally perfect, practically useless.

Prevention strategy: Make funding a checklist-driven task with proofs:

- *Real estate:* record a deed into the trust; update insurance.

- *Bank/brokerage:* open trust-titled accounts or retitle existing ones.
- *Life insurance/retirement:* coordinate beneficiary designations (often to the trust or subtrust, if appropriate).
- *Business interests:* update operating agreements, stock ledgers, or assignment documents.

Revisit funding after major life events and new acquisitions.

10.2 Wrong Trustee

A trustee is not a figurehead; they are the engine that drives the trust. One of the most damaging mistakes is appointing a trustee based on emotion or birth order rather than competence.

How it breaks: An overwhelmed or biased trustee misses deadlines, mismanages investments, or favors one beneficiary. Lawsuits follow; value and family goodwill are burned.

Example: A father chose his eldest son "because he's the oldest," ignoring the son's debt problems. The son "borrowed" from the trust, never repaid, and the siblings sued. Legal fees consumed what the trust was meant to preserve.

Prevention strategy: Choose trustees for integrity, organization, and willingness to get advice. If family dynamics are tense or assets are complex, consider a professional or institutional trustee. Being loved is not the same as being qualified.

10.3 DIY Pitfalls

Online forms can be helpful for simple plans, but state law is technical and unforgiving.

Risks:

- Missing protective clauses (e.g., spendthrift), leading to exposure to creditors.
- Ambiguities that cause banks or title companies to balk.
- Conflicts between the trust and beneficiary designations.

Prevention strategy: If you start with a template, pay for a review. A short attorney consult can catch issues that would cost far more later. The hybrid approach—DIY draft, professional polish—often hits the sweet spot.

10.4 Failing to Update

Life changes; documents must, too. Marriages, divorces, births, deaths, new assets, and relocations all impact your plan. Laws also change.

Example: A woman named her then-husband as trustee and primary beneficiary in her thirties. Twenty years and a divorce later, she never updated the trust. When she died, the ex-husband inherited and the current family received nothing. Litigation followed.

Prevention strategy: Review every 3–5 years and after major events. Confirm trustees, beneficiaries, distribution standards, and funding are still right. Update pour-over wills, powers of attorney, and health directives at the same time.

10.5 Mismatches

A trust says one thing; account titles and beneficiary forms say another. The forms usually win.

Common collisions:

- Retirement account or insurance beneficiary forms that bypass the trust's carefully staged plan.
- Joint accounts with survivorship that

unintentionally disinherit others.

Prevention strategy: Inventory every account and policy. Match each title and designation to the plan. Re-check after provider mergers or platform changes (forms get lost).

10.6 Overlooking Taxes

Even if taxes are not your main driver, ignoring the basics can be costly.

Misses to avoid:

- Failing to file for portability after the first spouse's death (when appropriate).
- Forgetting fiduciary income tax returns and K-1s.
- Ignoring the 65-day election that could shift prior-year income to beneficiaries.

Prevention strategy: Put a CPA on the team at death and for ongoing trusts. Calendar deadlines.

10.7 Too Vague

"Distribute as needed" invites conflict; "divide fairly" invites litigation.

Prevention strategy: Use clear standards (e.g.,

HEMS—health, education, maintenance, support) plus trustee discretion. Explain priorities (education first, housing second, luxury last). Provide examples.

10.8 Co-Trustee Chaos

Two or three co-trustees can balance perspectives—or produce stalemate.

Prevention strategy: If you use co-trustees, set tie-breakers and define roles (e.g., investment vs. distributions). Consider a professional as a third voice when siblings are co-trustees.

10.9 Real Estate Headaches

Property in a trust demands active management: taxes, insurance, tenants, repairs, and eventual sale.

Prevention strategy: Budget for upkeep, appoint a property manager, and give the trustee clear sell/hold guidance. Confirm homestead and community property nuances where relevant.

10.10 No Plan

Closely held businesses don't run themselves. A trust that inherits voting control without a buy–sell roadmap is a lawsuit waiting to happen.

Prevention strategy: Align operating agreements and shareholder agreements with the trust. Name who votes, how decisions are made, and what happens at death or disability. Keep key-person insurance current.

10.11 Digital Assets

Email, financial logins, cloud storage, social media, crypto—these can hold real value and real headaches.

Prevention strategy: Maintain a secure inventory of digital assets and access credentials. Reference applicable digital-access laws in your documents. Name who may access what.

10.12 Paperwork Gaps

Trustees who do not communicate or account lose beneficiary confidence—and cases.

Prevention strategy: Annual accounting, quarterly updates, and a predictable request-and-response process. Plain English cover letters help.

10.13 Three Fast Lessons

The "Fairness" Trap. Parents named all three children as co-trustees "to be fair." Every decision stalled. After months of deadlock, a professional trustee replaced them. Fair does not always mean equal authority.

The Vanishing Form. A bank merged and lost a beneficiary form. The default beneficiary received the account, not the trust. Periodic audits of titles and designations would have caught it.

The Tax Trip. A trustee retained income in the trust, pushing it into the highest bracket and triggering additional investment tax. A modest distribution before year-end (or via a timely election) would have shifted tax to lower-bracket beneficiaries.

10.14 Other Overlooked Mistakes

- **Overcomplicating the document.** Dense, rigid terms make administration brittle.
- **Ignoring situs and trustee location.** State income tax and oversight can hinge on these.
- **Neglecting insurance.** Liability and property policies must reflect trust ownership.

- **No successors named.** If your first-choice trustee can't serve, who steps in?

10.15 Takeaway

Most trust failures are not about obscure technicalities—they are about human oversights. An unfunded trust is useless. An unfit trustee can destroy harmony. Sloppy drafting or mismatched paperwork can collapse a plan under pressure. An outdated trust can betray your true intentions. Each of these mistakes is avoidable—if you remain engaged.

Think of your trust as a garden. Signing is planting. Funding is watering. Choosing the right trustee is healthy soil. Updating is pruning. Accounting is sunlight. Neglect any step, and the garden withers. Tend it, and it will flourish—providing shade, fruit, and shelter for the people you love. Your heirs deserve a plan that works not just in theory, but in practice. Avoid these mistakes, and your trust will deliver what you intended: peace, order, and protection.

Chapter 11

Florida Trusts

This chapter distills Florida-specific rules that most often matter in everyday trust planning and administration. It focuses on the Florida Trust Code and related statutes, with attention to execution formalities, homestead restrictions, spousal rights, creditor rules, and administration deadlines.

11.1 Florida Trust Law

Florida's trust law is primarily codified in the Florida Trust Code, Chapter 736, Florida Statutes. Related chapters include Chapter 732 for probate, Chapter 738 for principal and income, and Chapter 518 for investment standards. The Florida Constitution, particularly its homestead provision, also plays a critical role.

11.2 Trusts in Florida

Creation and Formalities

Florida recognizes multiple ways to create a trust. If a revocable trust is executed by a Florida domiciliary, any testamentary aspects (those disposing of property at or after death) are invalid unless the instrument is executed with the same formalities as a Florida will. This means the trust must be signed by the settlor in the presence of two attesting witnesses, who must also sign in the presence of each other and the settlor.

Governing Law and Venue

The Florida Trust Code provides jurisdiction to Florida courts over trust matters and specifies venue options, such as the county of the trust's principal place of administration or the county where a beneficiary resides.

11.3 Funding and Title Issues

Homestead in a Trust

Florida homestead property brings special rules. Homestead enjoys creditor protection but is subject to strict devise restrictions. A devise of homestead (including via trust) that violates the state constitution—such as when the owner is survived by a spouse or minor child—will fail. In that case, title passes under statutory defaults, often giving the surviving spouse a life estate and descendants the remainder. Florida statutes apply these restrictions directly to revocable trusts.

Beneficiary Designations and Joint Titling

Pay-on-death accounts, retirement plans, and insurance contracts pass outside probate by beneficiary designation. If the goal is to route them into a trust, designations must be updated carefully. Joint titling also passes outside probate and must be coordinated to align with trust planning.

11.4 Duties

Informing and Accounting

Trustees must keep qualified beneficiaries reasonably informed and provide annual accountings. The statute prescribes what an accounting must include, such as receipts, disbursements, and assets on hand.

Limitation Periods

A trustee's report or accounting that adequately discloses a matter can shorten the time for a beneficiary to bring a claim against the trustee. This makes careful and complete reporting important.

Prudent Investor Rule

Trustees in Florida must invest according to the prudent-investor standard, requiring diversification and care appropriate to the trust's purposes and beneficiaries. This standard is found in both the Trust Code and Chapter 518.

11.5 Spousal Rights

Elective Share

A surviving spouse of a Florida domiciliary may claim an elective share equal to thirty percent of the elective estate. The elective estate includes more than probate property; it often sweeps in revocable trust assets and other non-probate transfers. Trust planning in Florida must always account for this spousal right.

11.6 Creditor Claims

Spendthrift and Discretionary Trusts

Florida law enforces spendthrift clauses, which prevent beneficiaries from assigning interests and shield assets from most creditors. There are exceptions, including for certain claims such as support obligations. Discretionary trusts are also protected, though subject to statutory limits.

Settlor's Creditors

Creditors of a settlor may reach the maximum amount distributable to the settlor from a trust. After the settlor's death, revocable trust assets are generally subject to the settlor's debts and obligations, coordinated with the probate estate.

11.7 Notice of Obligations

When a Florida domiciliary dies with a revocable trust, the trustee must file a Notice of Trust in the probate court. Trust assets may be required to pay estate expenses and claims, in coordination with the personal representative.

11.8 Contests and Deadlines

Challenges to a revocable trust after death are subject to strict limitations periods. If a trustee sends proper notice with a copy of the trust, a beneficiary may have as little as six months to file a contest. Missing the deadline usually bars the claim.

11.9 Directed Trusts

Directed Trusts

Florida law permits directed trusts, in which a trustee may be directed by a trust director or advisor for investments or distributions. This allows specialized management while limiting trustee liability when properly drafted.

Decanting

Florida allows decanting: moving assets from one trust into another with modified terms, subject to statutory conditions and notice rules. This can modernize or correct old trusts without a court proceeding.

Nonjudicial Settlement Agreements

Interested parties may resolve certain trust matters by nonjudicial settlement agreement. This provides flexibility for administrative issues if all necessary parties are bound.

11.10 Income Rules

Florida's Principal and Income Act governs how trustees allocate receipts and disbursements between income and principal. Florida also allows a unitrust conversion, permitting trustees to distribute a fixed percentage (commonly 3–5%) of trust assets annually to income beneficiaries.

11.11 Nuts and Bolts

Acceptance, Resignation, and Removal

The Trust Code provides procedures for accepting trusteeship, resigning, or removing a trustee. Successor trustees step in as provided in the trust document, or by court if necessary.

Compensation

Trustees are entitled to reasonable compensation unless the trust provides otherwise. Florida courts may adjust fees that are unreasonably high or low.

11.12 Common Florida Pitfalls

- Executing a revocable trust without the formalities of a will: for Florida domiciliaries, two witnesses in each other's and the settlor's presence are required.
- Attempting to devise homestead in violation of spousal or minor-child restrictions.
- Forgetting to file the Notice of Trust after death.
- Assuming spendthrift protection is absolute; exceptions exist.

- Missing the six-month window for trust contests after statutory notice.

11.13 Practical Checklist

At Creation

1. Execute the trust with will-level formalities: settlor's signature and two attesting witnesses.
2. Coordinate beneficiary designations and joint accounts.
3. Address homestead carefully if placing in trust.
4. Draft pour-over will for safety.

At Settlor's Death

1. File Notice of Trust with probate court.
2. Coordinate with the personal representative regarding estate obligations.
3. Send statutory notices to beneficiaries to start limitations period.
4. Begin annual accountings and disclosures to qualified beneficiaries.
5. Review investments under prudent-investor

standards.

11.14 Closing Thought

Florida trust law offers powerful tools, but it is formalistic. Execution must follow will-level standards, homestead rules can override trust terms, and strict deadlines control contests and creditor claims. Careful drafting, timely filings, and regular communication keep Florida trusts effective and enforceable.

Chapter 12

Guardianships

Guardianship is one of the most important, and often least understood, elements of incapacity planning. A guardianship arises when a court appoints someone to manage the personal or financial affairs of an individual who can no longer do so for themselves. Guardianship can protect vulnerable people, but it is also intrusive, public, and sometimes contentious. Understanding how guardianships work, and how they interact with other planning tools such as powers of attorney, health care proxies, trusts, and advance directives, is essential to building a plan that minimizes risk and maximizes dignity.

12.1 What Is Guardianship?

A guardianship is a legal relationship created by a court. The "ward" (the person under guardianship) loses some or all of their ability to make decisions. The "guardian" is appointed to act in the ward's best interests.
Guardians may be appointed for:

- **The person:** managing daily life decisions, health care, living arrangements.
- **The property/estate:** managing finances, paying bills, investing assets.
- **Both:** a comprehensive guardianship covering all aspects of the ward's life.

Guardianship proceedings typically require medical evidence of incapacity and judicial findings. The process is formal, often involves hearings, and is supervised by the court on an ongoing basis.

12.2 Why Guardianships Exist

Guardianships are a last resort. They exist to protect individuals who cannot protect themselves and who have no less restrictive arrangement in place. Without them, vulnerable people could be financially exploited, left without care, or unable to make essential life decisions.

At the same time, courts emphasize that guardianships should remove no more rights than necessary, and alternatives should always be considered first.

12.3 Comparison

A power of attorney (POA) allows you to appoint someone to make financial decisions for you if you become incapacitated. If you have a valid POA, a guardianship for property is often unnecessary. The agent under a POA can pay bills, manage accounts, and handle legal transactions without court involvement.

Key differences:

- A POA is voluntary and created while you are competent. Guardianship is imposed by the court after incapacity is found.
- POA agents act without court supervision. Guardians act under court oversight and must often file accountings.
- A POA can be customized and revoked while competent. Guardianship is harder to alter and requires judicial intervention.

If a valid POA exists, courts usually defer to it unless the agent abuses authority or cannot act. Without a

POA, guardianship fills the vacuum.

12.4 Directives

Health care proxies (or medical powers of attorney) and living wills (advance directives) address medical decisions. A health care proxy lets you name someone to make health care decisions if you cannot. A living will sets out your wishes about end-of-life treatment. Together, these tools usually eliminate the need for a guardian of the person for medical matters.

Key points:

- If you have appointed a health care agent, a guardian is rarely needed for health care.
- If no agent exists, or if family members disagree, courts may appoint a guardian to make health decisions.
- Advance directives give guidance to both health care agents and guardians, ensuring your values are respected.

12.5 Guardianship vs. Trusts

Trusts are powerful incapacity planning tools. If you create and fund a revocable living trust and name successor trustees, those trustees can step in immediately to manage assets if you are incapacitated. This often eliminates the need for a financial guardianship.

Key distinctions:

- A trustee only controls trust assets. A guardian of property may control everything else (accounts not retitled, individually owned property).
- Courts can still appoint a guardian if assets are left outside the trust or if disputes arise about non-trust matters.
- Trusts provide more privacy and continuity; guardianships are court-supervised and public.

The best practice is to combine a trust with a durable power of attorney, ensuring nearly all assets are covered without court involvement.

12.6 Life Estates

A life estate deed allows someone (the life tenant) to live in or use property during their lifetime, with remainder beneficiaries receiving ownership afterward. If the life tenant becomes incapacitated, a guardian may be needed to make decisions about the property—such as maintaining it, renting it, or even selling it if necessary.

Important considerations:

- A trust can often handle real estate more flexibly than a life estate, avoiding the need for guardianship.
- If a life tenant has no power of attorney and cannot act, guardianship may be the only way to manage the property.

12.7 Other Advance Directives

Advance directives (such as do-not-resuscitate orders, psychiatric advance directives, or specific treatment instructions) guide both agents and guardians. They reduce uncertainty and conflict by clarifying your wishes. Without them, guardians and courts must guess—or worse, fight over—what you would have wanted.

12.8 Practical Examples

Example 1: An elderly man has a revocable trust and a durable POA. When he suffers a stroke, his successor trustee manages the trust assets and his agent pays bills not covered by the trust. No guardian is required.

Example 2: A middle-aged woman without a POA or trust is diagnosed with dementia. Her adult children disagree about her care. The court appoints a guardian of the person and property to resolve the impasse.

Example 3: A woman executes a health care proxy and a living will. Later incapacitated, her named health care agent makes decisions based on her written wishes. No guardianship proceeding is needed.

12.9 Still Necessary

Despite careful planning, guardianship may still be required in certain cases:

- When no valid POA, trust, or health care proxy exists.
- When there is serious family conflict or allegations of abuse by an agent or trustee.
- When oversight is needed because of complex circumstances (e.g., large estates, contested care decisions).

12.10 Takeaway

Guardianship is a vital safety net, but it is also the most restrictive and court-driven tool. Powers of attorney, trusts, health care proxies, and advance directives exist to prevent the need for guardianship. When they are in place and properly funded, guardianships are often unnecessary. But if planning has gaps, or if conflict arises, guardianship remains the backstop. The goal is to build a plan robust enough that the court never needs to intervene.

Chapter 13

Real Property

Real property law is a cornerstone of both estate planning and everyday transactions. It governs the land beneath our feet, the homes we live in, the businesses we build, and the legacy we pass on. This body of law stretches back centuries, blending common law traditions with modern statutory frameworks. It regulates how property is acquired, who owns it, how it can be divided, restricted, mortgaged, or transferred, and what happens when conflicts arise. While specific rules vary by state, the doctrines described here provide the essential framework for understanding real property rights in the United States, with particular attention to Florida where relevant.

13.1 Acquire Property

Property ownership arises in multiple ways, reflecting both voluntary transfers and involuntary shifts of title:

- **Sale (Purchase):** The most common method. A buyer and seller enter into a contract, negotiate terms, and consummate the transaction through delivery and acceptance of a deed. The deed must be properly executed, delivered, and often recorded.
- **Gift:** A voluntary transfer without consideration. To be effective, a gift of real property typically requires a deed executed with the same formalities as a sale, even though no payment is exchanged.
- **Devise:** When property passes through a valid will, the recipient is known as a devisee. The will must be admitted to probate for the devise to be effective.
- **Intestate Inheritance:** If a property owner dies without a will, the estate passes according to the state's intestacy statutes. In Florida, for example, a surviving spouse and descendants share the property in defined proportions.
- **Contractual Transfers:** Real estate can be

conveyed under contracts such as installment land contracts, lease-purchase agreements, or options to buy.

- **Lease and Rent:** Although not ownership in fee, leaseholds convey a present right of possession and use for a set term in exchange for rent. Long-term ground leases sometimes function like ownership interests.
- **Adverse Possession:** Title may be acquired without consent if someone occupies land openly, notoriously, continuously, and adversely for the statutory period (in Florida, generally seven years, with color of title or payment of taxes often required).

These diverse methods show that property rights are not static; they can shift by contract, by operation of law, or even by neglect.

13.2 Estates in Land

The law recognizes a spectrum of ownership interests, each carrying different rights and limitations:

- **Fee Simple Absolute:** The largest estate. It lasts forever, has no conditions, and is fully transferable. This is the default presumption in modern deeds.

- **Fee Simple Determinable:** Terminates automatically if a condition is broken ("so long as" language). The grantor holds a possibility of reverter.
- **Fee Simple Subject to Condition Subsequent:** Does not automatically terminate, but the grantor may exercise a right of entry if conditions are violated.
- **Life Estate:** Lasts for the life of a specified person. Upon that person's death, the property passes to the remainderman or reverts to the grantor. Life tenants must avoid waste and preserve the property's value.
- **Remainders:** Future interests that follow life estates. Vested remainders are certain to vest; contingent remainders depend on conditions precedent.
- **Executory Interests:** Future interests that cut short another estate. For example, "to A, but if B graduates law school, then to B."

Understanding these categories is crucial for estate planning. They determine who controls property now, who will control it in the future, and under what conditions.

13.3 Concurrent Ownership

Multiple people may own the same property together. The form of concurrent ownership shapes rights of survivorship, partition, and creditor access:

- **Tenancy in Common:** Each tenant owns a fractional, undivided share. Shares may be unequal, freely transferable, and devisable by will. No survivorship rights exist.
- **Joint Tenancy:** Each tenant has an equal share with right of survivorship. Upon death, a joint tenant's interest passes automatically to the survivors. It requires the four unities: time, title, interest, and possession. Severance (by sale, mortgage, or partition) can destroy the joint tenancy.
- **Tenancy by the Entirety:** Special to married couples in some states, including Florida. Neither spouse can unilaterally sever; survivorship applies. It offers strong creditor protection since only joint creditors may reach the property.

These distinctions often determine whether heirs inherit property directly or whether it bypasses probate altogether.

13.4 Statutory Spousal Rights

Property rights are also shaped by statutory protections and limitations:

- **Dower and Curtesy:** At common law, widows and widowers received life estates in portions of the decedent's property. Florida has abolished these, replacing them with elective share rights.
- **Pretermitted Shares:** Statutes protect spouses or children unintentionally omitted from a will, giving them default shares of the estate.
- **Elective Share:** In Florida, a surviving spouse may claim 30% of the elective estate, which includes probate and certain non-probate assets such as revocable trusts.
- **Community Property:** States like California treat property acquired during marriage as jointly owned. Florida is not a community property jurisdiction, but residents from such states may bring those rights with them.
- **Encumbrances:** Mortgages, tax liens, judgment liens, and restrictive covenants encumber property. These cloud title and restrict transfer.
- **Easements:** Nonpossessory rights allowing one

party to use another's land. They can be appurtenant (benefiting a parcel) or in gross (personal to a party). Easements may arise by express grant, implication, necessity, or prescription.

- **Judgment Liens:** When a creditor wins a judgment, it may attach to the debtor's property. This lien must be satisfied before sale or refinance.

13.5 Related Doctrines

- **Mortgages:** In lien-theory states like Florida, the borrower retains title while the lender has a lien. Foreclosure enforces the lien upon default.
- **Deeds of Trust/Mortgage Deeds:** Used in some states, these involve a trustee holding title as security until repayment.
- **Zoning:** Local ordinances regulate land use (residential, commercial, industrial). Property owners may seek variances or conditional use permits.
- **Restrictive Covenants:** Private agreements limiting use (e.g., no commercial activity). Often enforced by homeowners' associations.

- **Licenses:** Mere permissions to enter or use land, revocable at will (e.g., a ticket to a sports event).

13.6 Title and Recordation

Ownership depends on clear title, free of disputes or defects:

- **Ejectment:** Lawsuit to remove unlawful occupants.
- **Quiet Title:** Court action to establish clear ownership, removing competing claims.
- **Specific Performance:** In real estate contracts, courts often compel performance because each parcel is unique.
- **Recordation:** Recording deeds and liens protects against subsequent purchasers.
- **Chain of Title:** Historical ownership traced through recorded documents.
- **Race, Notice, Race-Notice Statutes:** Competing claim rules. Florida is a notice jurisdiction: bona fide purchasers without notice prevail over earlier unrecorded interests.

13.7 Medicaid Planning

- **Quitclaim Deed:** Transfers whatever interest the grantor has, with no warranties.
- **Warranty Deed:** Offers full covenants of seisin, right to convey, against encumbrances, quiet enjoyment, warranty, and further assurances.
- **Tax Deed:** Issued when property is sold for unpaid taxes after statutory procedures.
- **Descriptions of Property:** Legal descriptions may use metes and bounds, government surveys, or plat maps. Precision is essential to avoid disputes.
- **Medicaid Lookback:** Transfers of property for less than fair market value within five years of applying for Medicaid may result in disqualification or penalty periods.

13.8 Lending Issues

- **Second Mortgages:** Junior liens subordinate to first mortgages. Foreclosure may wipe them out if sale proceeds are insufficient.
- **Reverse Mortgages:** Allow seniors to convert home equity into income. Repayment typically

occurs upon death or sale.

- **Predatory Lending:** Loans with unconscionable terms, such as excessive fees or balloon payments. Federal and state laws restrict these practices.

13.9 Common-Interest Ownerships

- **Condominiums:** Unit owners own their units in fee simple, share common elements, and are governed by statutory frameworks like Florida's Condominium Act.
- **Homeowners' Associations (HOAs):** Govern subdivisions, enforce covenants, collect dues, and maintain shared areas.
- **Mobile Home Associations:** Special protections and regulations exist for mobile home parks.
- **Cooperatives:** Residents own shares in a corporation that owns the property, coupled with a proprietary lease.
- **Closings:** Real estate transactions culminate in closings: contracts, inspections, financing, title searches, settlement statements, and deed delivery.

- **Bona Fide Purchasers:** Buyers for value without notice of competing claims. BFPs are protected under notice and race-notice statutes.

13.10 Rule Against Perpetuities

Traditional Rule

At common law, no contingent interest is valid unless it must vest, if at all, no later than 21 years after some life in being at the creation of the interest. This rule prevents land from being tied up indefinitely by remote contingencies.

Florida's Rule Against Perpetuities

Florida has modified the doctrine. Under the Uniform Statutory Rule Against Perpetuities, an interest is valid if it satisfies the common-law test or if it actually vests within 90 years. Florida law also permits certain trusts (such as dynasty trusts) to extend for long durations, enabling more flexible planning.

13.11 Takeaway

Real property law is a dense and interconnected web of doctrines. From the way land is acquired—by purchase, gift, or adverse possession—to the intricate rules of estates, concurrent ownership, spousal rights, and encumbrances, every aspect matters. Add to this the layers of mortgages, zoning, title recording, deeds, and association governance, and it becomes clear why property law remains one of the most foundational areas of legal study and practice. Understanding these rules is essential for estate planners, homeowners, investors, and heirs alike, ensuring that property serves as a stable foundation rather than a source of conflict.

Chapter 14

Power of Attorney

A power of attorney (POA) is one of the most practical and widely used estate planning tools. Despite its name, it does not typically involve lawyers and does not turn the agent into an attorney-at-law. Instead, it establishes an agency relationship: one person (the **principal**) grants another person (the **agent** or **attorney-in-fact**) the legal authority to act on their behalf. This can be as narrow as signing one real estate deed, or as broad as managing all financial and personal matters.

In this chapter, we will examine the nature of a POA, the powers it can grant, the limits of those powers, and how it interacts with other planning tools such as wills, trusts, guardianships, and advance directives. We will also clarify the confusing terminology between "attorney-in-fact" and "attorney-at-law," and discuss why this distinction matters.

14.1 Attorney-in-Fact

The words "attorney" in the phrase "power of attorney" often cause misunderstanding.

- **Attorney-in-Fact:** This is the agent you appoint in a POA. They may be a spouse, child, friend, or professional fiduciary. They do not need a law degree, bar admission, or license to practice law. Their powers come only from the POA document itself. Their job is to act as your legal *stand-in*, carrying out transactions you could do yourself if you were present and able.
- **Attorney-at-Law:** This is a licensed lawyer authorized by the state to give legal advice, draft legal instruments, and represent clients in court. They must meet educational requirements, pass a bar exam, and maintain professional and ethical obligations.

Thus, appointing someone under a POA does not authorize them to give legal advice or represent you in court unless they are also a licensed attorney-at-law.

The title "attorney-in-fact" simply means agent.

14.2 Types of Powers of Attorney

There are several forms of POA, each serving different needs:

- **General POA:** Grants broad authority over most financial and personal matters. Often used for convenience, but it usually terminates if the principal becomes incapacitated.
- **Durable POA:** Continues in effect even if the principal loses capacity. This makes it the cornerstone of incapacity planning. Florida law requires specific statutory language for durability.
- **Limited or Special POA:** Grants authority for a single act or limited set of transactions—such as signing documents at a closing while the principal is abroad.
- **Springing POA:** Becomes effective upon the occurrence of a specified condition, usually incapacity. Florida no longer allows springing POAs; durable POAs are effective upon execution.
- **Military POA:** Special forms authorized under federal law, often used by service members

deploying overseas.

14.3 Powers Granted

A POA can be highly customized. Depending on its scope, an agent may be empowered to:

- Manage checking, savings, and brokerage accounts.
- Buy, sell, mortgage, or lease real estate.
- Pay everyday expenses and debts.
- File income tax and property tax returns.
- Operate or wind down a business.
- Manage retirement accounts and insurance policies.
- Apply for public benefits (Social Security, Medicaid, VA benefits).
- Handle digital assets such as email, cloud storage, and cryptocurrency.
- Make gifts, if explicitly authorized.
- Change beneficiary designations or create trusts, but only if expressly permitted by statute and initialed by the principal.

Florida and many other states require that certain "hot powers" (such as making gifts or changing beneficiaries) be expressly authorized in writing, often with the principal's initials next to the provision.

14.4 Limits of a POA

Despite its flexibility, a POA is not unlimited:

- **Ends at Death:** A POA is valid only during the principal's lifetime. It automatically terminates upon death. At that point, the will or trust governs.
- **No Power to Make or Revoke a Will:** An agent cannot execute, revoke, or amend a will for the principal.
- **Revocability:** A competent principal may revoke a POA at any time.
- **Fiduciary Duty:** Agents must act in good faith, avoid self-dealing, and keep the principal's interests foremost. Breach can result in liability.
- **Court Oversight Absent:** Unlike a guardianship, a POA agent is not supervised by the court unless challenged. Abuse can go undetected unless family or financial institutions intervene.

14.5 Other Planning Tools

POA vs. Will

- A will speaks only at death, while a POA is effective only during life.
- A will directs distribution of assets after death. A POA allows someone to manage assets and affairs while the principal is alive.
- A will always requires probate. A POA avoids court, operating privately.

POA vs. Trust

- A trust owns property in the name of the trustee; a POA agent acts in the principal's name.
- A trust continues after death; a POA ends at death.
- Trustees have defined fiduciary duties under trust law; POA agents act under agency law.

POA vs. Guardianship

- A POA is voluntary and executed by a competent person. Guardianship is imposed by a court after incapacity.

- Guardians are subject to ongoing judicial oversight; agents under POAs act privately.
- A properly drafted POA often avoids guardianship entirely.

POA vs. Health Care Proxy/Advance Directive

- Financial POAs cover money, property, and legal transactions. Health care proxies cover medical decisions.
- Advance directives set out treatment wishes. A POA agent must respect those instructions if also granted health care powers.

14.6 Practical Applications

- **Real Estate Closing:** A limited POA allows a family member to sign a deed for a seller stationed overseas.
- **Elder Care:** A durable POA enables an adult child to pay nursing home bills and manage Social Security checks for an incapacitated parent.

- **Business Management:** An entrepreneur grants a trusted partner POA authority to run daily operations during medical leave.
- **Incapacity Avoidance:** Without a POA, incapacity may require a costly guardianship proceeding. With one, the agent steps in seamlessly.

14.7 Risks and Abuse

Because POAs grant broad power with little oversight, abuse is a serious concern. Common problems include agents misusing funds, favoring themselves or certain heirs, or failing to keep records. Preventive measures include:

- Selecting trustworthy agents with financial competence.
- Requiring dual agents or co-signatures for major transactions.
- Notifying third parties (banks, accountants) of the scope of authority.
- Including oversight provisions, such as periodic accountings to another family member.

14.8 Florida-Specific

In Florida:

- POAs must be signed with the same formalities as a will: in the presence of two witnesses and a notary.
- Springing POAs are not recognized; durable POAs are effective immediately.
- "Hot powers" such as making gifts, creating trusts, or changing beneficiaries require explicit initialing.
- Agents must act as fiduciaries and can be held liable for abuse.

14.9 Takeaway

A power of attorney is not a substitute for a will or trust, but it is an indispensable complement. It ensures that someone can act for you in life, especially in the face of incapacity, without requiring court intervention. It does not survive death, but while you are alive it may be the single most important planning tool you can have. The attorney-in-fact is not a lawyer, but a stand-in, obligated to act in your best interests and limited by your instructions. Coordinated with wills, trusts, and health care directives, a POA provides continuity, autonomy, and peace of mind.

Chapter 15

Form A

This chapter contains the **Revocable Living Trust Form**. The layout below is margin-safe for a 6in×9in trim using fixed-width blanks (all under the 4.5in text width).

15.1 The Form

Date: ________________ **Year:** _____________

Grantor(s):

____

Initial Trustee(s):

____

Name of Trust:

____

The Grantor hereby transfers to the Trustee, in trust, the property described in **Schedule A**, to be held, administered, and distributed under this Agreement.

Article I — Name and Intent

This trust shall be known as the ______________________________________ (the "Trust"), created to provide efficient lifetime management, avoid probate, and distribute assets according to the Grantor's instructions.

Article II — Revocability and Amendments

1. During the Grantor's lifetime, this Trust is fully revocable and amendable by a signed writing delivered to the Trustee.
2. The Grantor may revoke or amend specific provisions without affecting the remainder.

Article III — Management During Grantor's Lifetime

1. The Trustee shall hold, manage, invest, and reinvest Trust assets for the Grantor's benefit.
2. Income shall be paid to, or applied for the benefit of, the Grantor. Principal may be distributed to the Grantor as needed.
3. If the Grantor becomes incapacitated (as certified in writing by a licensed physician), the Successor Trustee shall act immediately without court appointment.

Article IV — Trustee and Successor Trustee

Successor Trustee:

____

If the Trustee is unable or unwilling to serve, the Successor Trustee named above shall serve. If none is available, an adult beneficiary by majority may nominate a qualified successor.

Trustee Powers (summary): To invest and reinvest;

buy, sell, exchange, and lease property; maintain real estate; settle claims; employ professionals; allocate receipts and disbursements between income and principal; and perform all acts a prudent person would with respect to similar property.

Article V — Distributions Upon Death of Grantor

1. The Trustee shall pay legally enforceable debts, expenses of administration, and taxes associated with the Trust and the Grantor's estate to the extent permitted by law.
2. Tangible personal property shall be distributed according to any signed memorandum found with this Trust. If none exists, the Trustee may distribute in the Trustee's discretion, giving due regard to family sentiment.
3. The residue of the Trust Estate shall be distributed as follows:
   - **Beneficiary 1:** ________________________________ **Share:** ___________
   - **Beneficiary 2:**

________________________________ **Share:** ___________

- **Beneficiary 3:** ________________________________ **Share:** ___________

4. If a beneficiary is a minor or otherwise under a disability, the Trustee may hold such share in further trust and make discretionary distributions for health, education, maintenance, and support (HEMS) until distribution is appropriate.

Article VI — Spendthrift Protection

No beneficiary may voluntarily or involuntarily assign, anticipate, or encumber any interest in this Trust, and no such interest shall be subject to the claims of creditors or legal process, to the maximum extent allowed by law.

Article VII — Administrative Provisions

- The Trustee shall act with reasonable care, skill, and caution; may diversify investments consistent with the prudent investor standard.

- The Trustee may rely on advisors (legal, tax, investment) and pay reasonable fees.
- The Trustee shall keep reasonable records and provide periodic reports to current beneficiaries as required by law.
- The Trustee shall serve without bond unless otherwise required by law or the Grantor.

Article VIII — Governing Law

This Agreement shall be governed by the laws of

________________________________.

Article IX — Definitions and Miscellaneous

Headings are for convenience only. If any provision is invalid, the remainder shall be enforced. Singular includes plural as context requires.

IN WITNESS WHEREOF, the undersigned have executed this Revocable Living Trust Agreement as of the date first above written.

Grantor:

____

Date: ____________

Trustee:

____

Date: ____________

Witnesses

(Both witnesses sign in the presence of the Grantor and each other.)

Witness #1:

______________________________ Date: ____________

Witness #2:

______________________________ Date: ____________

Notary Acknowledgment

State: ____________ County: ____________ Date: ____________

Notary Public: ______________________

Schedule A — Trust Property

Attach pages as needed. Keep descriptions concise to stay within margins.

Real Estate (address):

____

Legal Description (attach if lengthy):

____

Bank Accounts (institution & last 4):

____

Brokerage/Investments:

____

Life Insurance (if ownership assigned to Trust):

____

Other Assets:

____

Funding Reminder: Record new deeds, retitle financial accounts to the Trust, and update beneficiary designations where appropriate. Keep confirmations with this Schedule.

15.2 Sample

Date: January 15 **Year:** 2025

Grantor(s): John Q. Smith

Initial Trustee(s): John Q. Smith

Name of Trust: The Smith Family Revocable Living Trust

The Grantor hereby transfers to the Trustee, in trust, the property described in **Schedule A**, to be held, administered, and distributed under this Agreement.

Article I — Name and Intent

This trust shall be known as the Smith Family Revocable Living Trust (the "Trust"), created to provide efficient lifetime management, avoid probate, and distribute assets according to the Grantor's instructions.

Article II — Revocability and Amendments

1. During the Grantor's lifetime, this Trust is fully revocable and amendable by a signed writing delivered to the Trustee.

2. The Grantor may revoke or amend specific provisions without affecting the remainder.

Article III — Management During Grantor's Lifetime

1. The Trustee shall hold, manage, invest, and reinvest Trust assets for the Grantor's benefit.
2. Income shall be paid to, or applied for the benefit of, the Grantor. Principal may be distributed to the Grantor as needed.
3. If the Grantor becomes incapacitated (as certified in writing by a licensed physician), the Successor Trustee shall act immediately without court appointment.

Article IV — Trustee and Successor Trustee

Successor Trustee: Jane R. Smith

If the Trustee is unable or unwilling to serve, the Successor Trustee named above shall serve. If none is available, an adult beneficiary by majority may nominate a qualified successor.

Trustee Powers (summary): To invest and reinvest; buy, sell, exchange, and lease property; maintain real estate; settle claims; employ professionals; allocate receipts and disbursements between income and principal; and perform all acts a prudent person would with respect to similar property.

Article V — Distributions Upon Death of Grantor

1. The Trustee shall pay legally enforceable debts, expenses of administration, and taxes associated with the Trust and the Grantor's estate.
2. Tangible personal property shall be distributed according to any signed memorandum.
3. The residue of the Trust Estate shall be distributed as follows:
    - **Beneficiary 1:** Jane R. Smith **Share:** 60%
    - **Beneficiary 2:** Michael Smith **Share:** 20%
    - **Beneficiary 3:** Sarah Smith **Share:** 20%
4. If a beneficiary is a minor, the Trustee may hold such share in further trust and make HEMS

distributions until age 25.

Article VI — Spendthrift Protection

No beneficiary may assign or encumber any interest in this Trust, and no such interest shall be subject to creditors' claims.

Article VII — Administrative Provisions

- The Trustee shall act with reasonable care, skill, and caution.
- The Trustee may hire advisors and pay reasonable fees.
- The Trustee shall provide periodic reports as required by law.
- The Trustee shall serve without bond.

Article VIII — Governing Law

This Agreement shall be governed by the laws of Florida.

Article IX — Definitions and Miscellaneous

Headings are for convenience only. Invalid provisions do not affect the remainder.

IN WITNESS WHEREOF, the undersigned have executed this Revocable Living Trust Agreement as of the date first above written.

Grantor:

John Q. Smith

Date: January 15, 2025

Trustee:

John Q. Smith

Date: January 15, 2025

Witnesses

Witness #1: Mary Johnson Date: January 15, 2025

Witness #2: Robert Johnson Date: January 15, 2025

Notary Acknowledgment

State: Florida County: Broward Date: January 15, 2025

Notary Public: Lisa M. Clark

15.3 Schedule A — Trust Property

Real Estate (address): 123 Main Street, Fort Lauderdale, FL

Legal Description: See attached Exhibit A

Bank Accounts: ABC Bank, Account #1234

Brokerage/Investments: Fidelity Brokerage, Account #5678

Life Insurance: XYZ Life, Policy #4321

Other Assets: Household furnishings, vehicle (2018 Toyota Camry)

Chapter 16

Form B

This chapter presents a sample **Irrevocable Living Trust** form. Unlike the revocable trust, this type cannot be undone once created, except in rare and limited situations allowed by law.

Key features of an irrevocable trust include:

- Transfer of ownership: once assets are placed in the trust, the grantor no longer owns or controls them.
- Tax treatment: often used to minimize estate or gift taxes.
- Asset protection: shields property from creditors and certain lawsuits.

- Planning for care: sometimes used to qualify for Medicaid or other benefits.
- Insurance planning: can hold life insurance policies outside the grantor's taxable estate.

Practical considerations:

- Changes are difficult: amendments require court approval or agreement of all beneficiaries.
- Trustee independence: the trustee must manage the property for the benefit of others, not the grantor.
- Reporting: may require separate tax filings and careful accounting.
- Legal drafting: professional oversight is strongly recommended to avoid unintended results.

Below is a structured outline of an **Irrevocable Living Trust Form**:

1. **Title and Declaration**
   "This Irrevocable Living Trust is created on [date] by [grantor name], hereafter referred to as Grantor."
2. **Trust Property**
   Description of the property transferred into the trust (real estate, securities, insurance policies,

etc.).

3. **Trustee Appointment**
   Name of the trustee(s), with powers to manage and invest trust property.

4. **Beneficiaries**
   Identification of persons or entities who will benefit from the trust.

5. **Distributions**
   Rules for income and principal distributions, either during the grantor's life or at death.

6. **Trustee Powers**
   Authority to buy, sell, invest, and otherwise manage assets, subject to fiduciary duties.

7. **Irrevocability Clause**
   Statement that the trust cannot be amended, revoked, or terminated by the grantor.

8. **Signatures and Notarization**
   Execution by the grantor and trustee(s), with notary acknowledgment.

Sample Form Language (for illustration only):

IRREVOCABLE LIVING TRUST AGREEMENT

This Irrevocable Living Trust Agreement ("Agreement") is made this ______________ day of ______________, 20____, by and between ______________________ ("Grantor") and ______________________ ("Trustee").

1. Declaration of Trust. The Grantor hereby irrevocably transfers, assigns, and delivers to the Trustee all property described in *Schedule A*, to be held in trust under the terms set forth herein.

2. Beneficiaries. The beneficiaries of this trust shall be: ______________________.

3. Distributions. The Trustee shall distribute income and/or principal to the beneficiaries as follows:

__________________________.

4. Trustee Powers. The Trustee shall have the authority to invest, reinvest, sell, lease, and otherwise manage the trust assets in accordance with fiduciary standards.

5. Irrevocability. This trust is irrevocable. The Grantor expressly waives all rights and powers to alter, amend, revoke, or terminate this Agreement.

6. Signatures.

Grantor: ______________________________

Trustee: ______________________________

Date: ______________________________

Notary Acknowledgment Attached

Caution: This sample is for educational purposes. State-specific requirements vary, and professional legal advice is essential.

Chapter 17

Form C

This chapter provides a sample **Trust Revocation Form**, used to terminate a previously created **Revocable Living Trust**. Once executed, the revocation cancels the trust and returns ownership of the trust property to the grantor.

Key purposes:

- End the trust relationship created under a revocable trust.
- Reclaim direct ownership of assets.
- Clarify to beneficiaries and third parties that the trust no longer exists.

- Provide a recordable document for use with banks, title companies, and courts.

Important points to include:

- **Grantor identification:** full legal name and address of the person revoking the trust.
- **Trust reference:** name of the original trust and the date it was created.
- **Revocation statement:** clear declaration that the trust is revoked in its entirety.
- **Execution:** signature of the grantor, plus required witnesses and notary acknowledgment.

Below is a structured outline of a **Trust Revocation Form**:

1. **Title and Heading**
   "Revocation of Revocable Living Trust."
2. **Identification of Grantor**
   Full name and address of the person revoking the trust.
3. **Reference to Trust**
   Title and date of the trust agreement being revoked.
4. **Revocation Language**

Clear statement revoking the trust in full and terminating all powers and duties.

5. **Disposition of Assets**
   Statement that property held in trust reverts to the grantor or as otherwise directed.

6. **Signatures and Witnesses**
   Grantor's signature, witness attestation, and notary acknowledgment.

Sample Form Language (for illustration only):

REVOCATION OF REVOCABLE LIVING TRUST

I, ______________________________, residing at ______________________________, hereby revoke in its entirety the trust agreement known as the [**Title of Trust**], originally executed on _______________, 20_____.

All property held in the name of said trust shall henceforth be owned by me individually, free of the trust. This revocation is effective immediately.

Signature:

______________________________ Date:

____

Witnesses:

____

____

Notary Acknowledgment: Subscribed and sworn before me on this ______________ day of ______________, 20____.

Notary Public:

____

Caution: Revocation should be formally recorded and communicated to trustees, beneficiaries, and relevant institutions to avoid disputes.

Chapter 18

Form D

This chapter presents a sample **Living Trust Amendment Form**. An amendment is used when the grantor wishes to change specific provisions of an existing **Revocable Living Trust** without replacing or revoking the entire document.

Common uses:

- Updating successor trustee designations.
- Changing distribution percentages or terms.
- Adding or removing beneficiaries.
- Revising administrative provisions to reflect current needs.

Key considerations:

- The amendment must clearly reference the original trust, including its title and date.
- Each amendment should be signed and notarized with the same formality as the original trust.
- Multiple amendments can create confusion; in some cases, a restatement of trust may be more efficient.
- Only the grantor(s) with amendment power may execute the amendment.

Structured outline of a **Living Trust Amendment Form**:

1. **Title and Heading**
   "Amendment to Revocable Living Trust."
2. **Reference to Original Trust**
   Full title and date of the trust agreement being amended.
3. **Amendment Language**
   Clear description of which section(s) are being changed, deleted, or replaced.
4. **Substitute Provisions**
   New text to replace or modify the specified sections.

5. **Confirmation of No Other Changes**
   Statement that all other provisions of the trust remain in effect.

6. **Signatures and Notarization**
   Execution by the grantor(s), acknowledgment by witnesses, and notarization.

Sample Form Language (for illustration only):

> **AMENDMENT TO REVOCABLE LIVING TRUST**
>
> I, ______________________________, residing at ______________________________, the Grantor of the trust titled [**Title of Trust**], dated ______________, 20_____, hereby make this amendment to the trust.
>
> **1. Identification of Amended Section.** The section of the trust concerning ______________________________ is hereby amended.
>
> **2. New Provision.** The following language shall replace the prior provision:
>
> ____
>
> **3. No Other Changes.** Except as specifically amended herein, all provisions of

the trust remain in full force and effect.

Signature:

______________________________ Date:

____

Witnesses:

____

____

Notary Acknowledgment: Subscribed and sworn before me on this _______________ day of _______________, 20____.

Notary Public:

____

Caution: Successive amendments can complicate administration; when changes become numerous, a full restatement is often clearer.

Chapter 19

Form E

This chapter presents a sample **Special Needs Trust** template. This trust is designed to provide for the supplemental care of a disabled beneficiary while preserving their eligibility for government benefits such as Medicaid or Supplemental Security Income (SSI).

Key features:

- Provides supplemental (not substitute) support — intended to enhance quality of life, not replace public assistance.
- Grants trustee full discretion over distributions, preventing the beneficiary from having direct control over assets.

- Contains restrictions to avoid disqualification from needs-based government benefits.
- Often used by parents, guardians, or family members planning for long-term care.

Important considerations:

- **Public benefits rules:** The trust must be carefully drafted to comply with Medicaid and SSI regulations.
- **Trustee selection:** The trustee must act prudently, balancing the beneficiary's needs with benefit eligibility.
- **Permitted expenditures:** Funds are typically used for items not covered by government benefits, such as education, recreation, transportation, or special therapies.
- **Irrevocability:** Special needs trusts are often irrevocable to satisfy eligibility requirements.

Structured outline of a **Special Needs Trust**:

1. **Title and Declaration**
   "Special Needs Trust Agreement" created by the grantor for the benefit of a named disabled individual.

2. **Identification of Parties**
   Grantor, trustee, and beneficiary clearly identified.
3. **Trust Purpose**
   States that the purpose is to supplement, not replace, government benefits.
4. **Trust Property**
   Description of property contributed to the trust.
5. **Trustee Powers and Discretion**
   Trustee has sole discretion regarding distributions, with explicit limits to preserve benefit eligibility.
6. **Prohibited Uses**
   Statement that trust funds cannot be used for basic support covered by government benefits (e.g., food and shelter).
7. **Termination and Remainder**
   Provides instructions for what happens to remaining assets upon the beneficiary's death.
8. **Signatures and Notarization**
   Grantor and trustee execute the agreement with required witnesses and notary.

Sample Form Language (for illustration only):

SPECIAL NEEDS TRUST

AGREEMENT

This Special Needs Trust Agreement ("Agreement") is made this ____________ day of ______________, 20____, by and between ________________________ ("Grantor") and ________________________ ("Trustee"), for the benefit of ________________________ ("Beneficiary").

1. Purpose. This trust is established to provide supplemental benefits for the Beneficiary, who is disabled, while preserving eligibility for Medicaid, SSI, and other government assistance programs.

2. Trust Property. The Grantor hereby transfers and delivers to the Trustee the property described in *Schedule A*, to be held in trust under this Agreement.

3. Distributions. The Trustee may, in their sole discretion, make distributions for the benefit of the Beneficiary to provide comforts, goods, or services not otherwise provided by public assistance.

4. Restrictions. No part of the trust shall be used for the Beneficiary's basic support (food, shelter, or medical care) when such support would disqualify the Beneficiary from government benefits.

5. Termination. Upon the death of the Beneficiary, the Trustee shall distribute the remaining trust property as follows: ______________________________.

Signatures:

Grantor: ______________________________ Date: _____________

Trustee: ______________________________ Date: _____________

Witnesses:

____

____

Notary Acknowledgment: Subscribed and sworn before me on this _____________ day of _____________, 20____.

Notary Public:

____

Caution: Because benefit eligibility rules are complex and vary by state, a special needs trust should always be drafted or reviewed by a qualified professional.

Chapter 20

Form F

This chapter provides a sample **Pet Trust Form**. A pet trust ensures that pets are properly cared for in the event of the owner's death or incapacity. It provides legal authority for a designated caregiver to manage funds and make decisions for the welfare of the animals.

Core features:

- Identification of each pet covered by the trust.
- Appointment of a caregiver responsible for daily care.
- Allocation of funds to cover food, veterinary care, housing, and related expenses.

- Provision for a successor caregiver if the primary caregiver cannot serve.
- Oversight by a trustee to ensure funds are used properly.

Practical considerations:

- Trust duration is typically for the lifetime of the named pets.
- Funds should be reasonable to avoid legal challenges from heirs.
- Successor caregiver planning is essential in case the first choice is unable or unwilling.
- Remainder beneficiaries should be named to receive unused funds after the pets' lifetimes.

Structured outline of a **Pet Trust**:

1. **Title and Declaration**
   "Pet Trust Agreement" created by the grantor for the care of identified pets.
2. **Identification of Pets**
   Names, breeds, descriptions, or microchip numbers for clarity.
3. **Caregiver Appointment**

Naming of the individual(s) who will provide day-to-day care.

4. **Funding the Trust**
   Specific allocation of funds for pet care.
5. **Trustee Appointment**
   Appointment of a trustee to manage funds and oversee the caregiver.
6. **Successor Caregiver and Trustee**
   Alternatives if the original caregiver or trustee cannot serve.
7. **Permitted Expenditures**
   Food, medical care, grooming, boarding, and related expenses.
8. **Termination and Remainder**
   Instructions for distribution of any remaining funds after the pets' lifetimes.
9. **Signatures and Notarization**
   Execution by the grantor, with required witnesses and notary acknowledgment.

Sample Form Language (for illustration only):

PET TRUST AGREEMENT

This Pet Trust Agreement ("Agreement") is

made this ______________ day of ______________, 20____, by ______________________ ("Grantor"), for the benefit of the pets described herein.

1. Identification of Pets. This trust covers the following pets:

____.

2. Caregiver Appointment. The Grantor appoints ____________________________ as the primary caregiver. If unable or unwilling to serve, the successor caregiver shall be ____________________________.

3. Trustee Appointment. The Grantor appoints ____________________________ as Trustee to oversee and manage funds for the pets' benefit.

4. Funding. The Grantor transfers the sum of ______________ to the Trustee, to be used solely for the care and maintenance of the pets.

5. Permitted Expenditures. Funds may be used for food, veterinary care, grooming, housing, and other needs to ensure the pets' well-being.

6. Termination. Upon the death of the last surviving pet covered by this trust, any remaining funds shall be distributed to

______________________________.

Signatures:

Grantor:

____________________________________ Date:

____

Trustee:

____________________________________ Date:

____

Witnesses:

____

____

Notary Acknowledgment: Subscribed and sworn before me on this _______________ day of _______________, 20_____.

Notary Public:

____

Caution: Pet trusts must comply with state statutes, which often set limits on duration and funding.

Consultation with a legal professional is recommended.

Chapter 21

Form G

This chapter provides both a sample **Last Will & Testament** and a **Pour-Over Will**. Together, these forms ensure that any property not already titled in the trust during life is transferred ("poured over") into the trust upon death.

Key features:

- Establishes a traditional Last Will & Testament for basic estate matters.
- Provides a pour-over clause so that residual property flows into the living trust.
- Names an executor (personal representative) to handle estate administration.

- Includes standard will provisions (payment of debts, funeral expenses, residuary clause).
- Prevents assets from being unintentionally left outside of the trust.

Important considerations:

- The pour-over will must be properly executed with the same formalities as a will under state law.
- The living trust referenced must already exist at the time of death.
- Assets passing through the pour-over will may still be subject to probate.
- Coordination with beneficiary designations (retirement accounts, life insurance, etc.) is essential.

Structured outline of a **Last Will & Testament with Pour-Over Will**:

1. **Title and Declaration**
   "Last Will and Testament of [Name]" including statement of domicile.
2. **Appointment of Executor**
   Naming of executor/personal representative and successor.

3. **Payment of Debts and Expenses**
   Directions for funeral, debts, and expenses.

4. **Specific Bequests (optional)**
   Items of personal property, cash gifts, or charitable bequests.

5. **Pour-Over Clause**
   Directs the residuary estate to the trustee of the grantor's living trust.

6. **Guardian for Minor Children (if applicable)**
   Appointment of guardian(s) for minor children.

7. **Residuary Clause**
   Any remaining estate property is distributed via the living trust.

8. **Execution and Attestation**
   Grantor's signature, witness signatures, and notary (if required).

Sample Form Language (for illustration only):

> **LAST WILL AND TESTAMENT**
>
> I, ______________________________, residing at ______________________________, being of sound mind, declare this to be my Last Will and Testament, hereby revoking all prior

wills and codicils.

1. Executor. I appoint ______________________________ as Executor of my estate. If they cannot serve, I appoint ______________________________ as successor.

2. Debts and Expenses. I direct my Executor to pay all just debts, funeral expenses, and costs of estate administration.

3. Specific Bequests. I give the following: ____.

4. Pour-Over Clause. I give all the rest, residue, and remainder of my estate to the trustee of the [**Title of Living Trust**], dated _______________, 20_____, to be held, administered, and distributed as part of that trust.

5. Guardian for Minor Children (if applicable). I appoint ______________________________ as guardian of my minor children.

Execution:

In witness whereof, I have hereunto set my

hand this ______________ day of ______________, 20____.

Testator:

____

Witnesses:

The foregoing instrument was signed in our presence by ____________________________, who declared it to be their Last Will and Testament. We, at the request of the testator and in their presence, and in the presence of each other, sign our names as witnesses.

Witness:

____

Witness:

____

Notary Acknowledgment (if required):
Subscribed and sworn before me this ______________ day of ______________, 20____.

Notary Public:

____

Caution: While a pour-over will provides a safety net, assets not transferred to the trust during life may still pass through probate before reaching the trust.

Chapter 22

Form H

This chapter presents a sample **Advance Healthcare Directive / Living Will**. This form allows an individual to state medical treatment preferences in the event of incapacity and to appoint a trusted person to make healthcare decisions on their behalf.

Key features:

- Allows the declarant to accept or refuse life-sustaining treatment under specific conditions.
- Provides direction regarding pain management, comfort care, and palliative treatment.
- Offers the opportunity to state organ and tissue donation preferences.

- Appoints a healthcare surrogate (agent) to make decisions when the declarant is unable.

Important considerations:

- Must comply with state statutory requirements for validity.
- Typically requires signatures of the declarant and witnesses, sometimes notarization.
- The healthcare surrogate should be someone trusted to follow the declarant's wishes.
- Regular review is important to keep the directive current with medical preferences.

Structured outline of an **Advance Healthcare Directive / Living Will**:

1. **Title and Declaration**
   "Advance Healthcare Directive" or "Living Will" statement by the declarant.
2. **Life-Sustaining Treatment Preferences**
   Instructions about resuscitation, artificial nutrition and hydration, ventilators, etc.
3. **Pain Management and Comfort Care**
   Directives for palliative and hospice care, regardless of life expectancy.

4. **Organ Donation Preferences**
   Authorization for organ or tissue donation, if desired.

5. **Appointment of Healthcare Surrogate**
   Naming of primary and alternate agents authorized to make healthcare decisions.

6. **Effective Date and Revocation**
   Statement about when the directive takes effect and how it can be revoked.

7. **Signatures and Witnesses**
   Declarant's signature, witness signatures, and notary if required by law.

Sample Form Language (for illustration only):

> **ADVANCE HEALTHCARE DIRECTIVE / LIVING WILL**
>
> I, ______________________________, residing at ______________________________, being of sound mind, make this directive regarding my healthcare preferences.
>
> **1. Life-Sustaining Treatment.** If I am terminally ill, permanently unconscious, or in an end-stage condition, I direct that life-sustaining treatment

[continue / not be continued] according to my stated wishes.

2. Pain Management and Comfort Care. I direct that I be provided with treatment to relieve pain and ensure comfort, even if it may shorten my life.

3. Organ Donation. Upon my death, I [do / do not] authorize the donation of my organs and tissues for transplantation or research.

4. Healthcare Surrogate. I appoint ______________________________ as my healthcare surrogate to make medical decisions if I am unable. If this person cannot serve, I appoint ______________________________ as successor.

5. Effectiveness and Revocation. This directive becomes effective upon my incapacity. I may revoke it at any time by written or oral notice.

Signature:

____________________________________ Date:

____

Witnesses:

____

____

Notary Acknowledgment (if required):

Subscribed and sworn before me this

______________ day of ______________,

20_____.

Notary Public:

____

Caution: Advance directives are subject to specific state laws. Local statutes should be consulted to ensure compliance and enforceability.

Chapter 23

Form I

This chapter presents a sample **Durable Power of Attorney (POA)**. A Durable Power of Attorney authorizes a trusted agent (attorney-in-fact) to act on behalf of the principal in financial and legal matters. Its durability means that the authority remains in effect even if the principal becomes incapacitated.

Key features:

- Authorizes an agent to handle banking, investments, and financial accounts.
- Empowers the agent to manage real estate transactions, leases, and maintenance.
- Allows bill payment, tax filings, and debt

management.

- Provides authority to apply for and manage government benefits.
- May be tailored to grant general or limited powers.

Important considerations:

- The agent must act as a fiduciary, in the best interest of the principal.
- Some powers (e.g., gifting, changing beneficiaries) require explicit language to be valid.
- Execution requirements vary by state, often requiring witnesses or notarization.
- The principal can revoke the POA at any time while competent.

Structured outline of a **Durable Power of Attorney**:

1. **Title and Declaration**
   "Durable Power of Attorney" created by the principal.
2. **Identification of Parties**
   Names and addresses of the principal and agent(s).
3. **Grant of Authority**
   Scope of powers given to the agent, with optional limitations.

4. **Durability Clause**
   Statement that the POA remains effective despite the principal's incapacity.

5. **Successor Agent**
   Appointment of an alternate agent if the first cannot serve.

6. **Effective Date**
   Immediate effectiveness or "springing" upon incapacity.

7. **Revocation**
   Principal's right to revoke the POA at any time while competent.

8. **Signatures and Notarization**
   Execution by the principal, acknowledgment by witnesses, and notarization.

Sample Form Language (for illustration only):

DURABLE POWER OF ATTORNEY

I, ______________________________, residing at ______________________________, designate ______________________________ ("Agent") to act as my attorney-in-fact.

1. Grant of Authority. I grant my Agent

the authority to manage my financial, legal, and personal affairs, including but not limited to:

- Banking, investments, and securities.
- Real estate purchases, sales, and management.
- Bill payment, tax filings, and debt management.
- Applications for and management of government benefits.

2. Durability. This power of attorney shall not be affected by my subsequent incapacity.

3. Successor Agent. If my Agent cannot serve, I appoint ______________________________ as successor Agent.

4. Effective Date. This power of attorney is effective [immediately / upon my incapacity].

5. Revocation. I retain the right to revoke this document at any time while competent.

Signature:

____ Date:

____

Witnesses:

____

____

Notary Acknowledgment: Subscribed and sworn before me on this _________________ day of _________________, 20_____.

Notary Public:

____

Caution: A Durable Power of Attorney grants broad powers that may be misused. Only a trusted individual should be appointed as Agent.

Chapter 24

Form J

This chapter provides a sample **Minor Child Medical Consent Form**. This form authorizes another adult, such as a grandparent, relative, or babysitter, to consent to medical treatment for a minor child when the parent or legal guardian is unavailable.

Key purposes:

- Ensures timely medical care for a child in emergencies or routine visits when a parent cannot be present.
- Provides legal authority to healthcare providers to rely on the consent of the designated adult.
- Offers peace of mind to parents and caregivers by

clarifying responsibilities.

Important considerations:

- The form should clearly identify the child and the authorized adult.
- Consent may cover both routine and emergency treatment, but parents may limit the scope.
- Effective dates should be specified (e.g., during a vacation or indefinitely until revoked).
- Many states require notarization for broader acceptance by medical providers.

Structured outline of a **Minor Child Medical Consent Form**:

1. **Title and Declaration**
   "Minor Child Medical Consent Form."
2. **Identification of Child**
   Full legal name, date of birth, and other identifying information.
3. **Identification of Consenting Adult**
   Name, relationship to child, and contact information.
4. **Scope of Consent**

Specific authorization for routine care, emergency treatment, or both.

5. **Effective Dates**
   Beginning and ending dates of the authorization.

6. **Parent/Guardian Signatures**
   Signatures of legal parent(s) or guardian(s).

7. **Notary Acknowledgment**
   Optional but recommended for validity and acceptance.

Sample Form Language (for illustration only):

MINOR CHILD MEDICAL CONSENT FORM

I, ______________________________,
parent/legal guardian of:

Child's Full Name:
______________________________ Date of Birth: ______________________________

Hereby authorize:

Name of Adult:
____

Relationship to Child:
____

Address/Phone:

____

to consent to routine or emergency medical care, including diagnostic procedures, anesthesia, surgery, and hospital admission, as deemed necessary by a licensed healthcare provider.

This consent is valid from _______________ to _______________.

Signatures:

Parent/Guardian:

___________________________________ Date:

____

Parent/Guardian (if applicable):

___________________________________ Date:

____

Notary Acknowledgment (recommended): Subscribed and sworn before me on this _______________ day of _______________, 20_____.

Notary Public:

____

Caution: While widely accepted, some hospitals or providers may require their own consent forms in addition to this document.

Chapter 25

Form K

This chapter presents a sample **HIPAA Authorization Form**. This form allows an individual to authorize designated persons to access and receive their protected health information (PHI) from healthcare providers, as required by the Health Insurance Portability and Accountability Act (HIPAA).

Key purposes:

- Grants permission for doctors, hospitals, and insurers to share medical information with named individuals.
- Often used to allow family members, caregivers, or agents under a healthcare power of attorney to

obtain records.

- Ensures compliance with federal privacy laws so providers do not face penalties for disclosure.

Important considerations:

- The authorization must clearly identify the individual, the authorized recipients, and the scope of information disclosed.
- The form should state the purpose of the disclosure (e.g., treatment, billing, legal).
- The individual has the right to revoke the authorization in writing at any time.
- A HIPAA authorization generally expires on a set date or event unless otherwise stated.

Structured outline of a **HIPAA Authorization Form**:

1. **Title and Declaration**
   "HIPAA Authorization for Release of Medical Information."
2. **Identification of Patient**
   Full legal name, date of birth, and contact details.
3. **Authorized Recipients**
   Names and contact information of those allowed to receive PHI.

4. **Scope of Information**
   Types of information disclosed (general medical, mental health, billing, etc.).

5. **Purpose of Disclosure**
   Statement of reason (treatment, insurance, legal, personal).

6. **Expiration**
   Date or event upon which authorization expires.

7. **Revocation Rights**
   Statement that authorization may be revoked in writing at any time.

8. **Signatures**
   Patient's signature, date, and witness or notary if required.

Sample Form Language (for illustration only):

> **HIPAA AUTHORIZATION FOR RELEASE OF MEDICAL INFORMATION**
>
> Patient Name: ______________________________ Date of Birth: ______________________________
>
> **1. Authorization.** I authorize the release of

my protected health information to the following person(s): Name(s):

____

2. Scope of Information. This authorization applies to: [all medical records / specific records].

3. Purpose of Disclosure. The information is to be disclosed for the following purpose:

____________________________.

4. Expiration. This authorization shall expire on ______________ or upon the occurrence of

____________________________.

5. Revocation. I understand I may revoke this authorization in writing at any time, except to the extent it has already been relied upon.

Signature of Patient:

________________________________ Date:

____

Witness/Notary (if required):

____

Caution: HIPAA authorizations must meet specific federal requirements. Some providers may require their own version of this form in addition to a general authorization.

Chapter 26

Form L

This chapter presents a sample **Financial Information Release Authorization**. This form allows an individual to authorize a financial institution or advisor to disclose account details, statements, or related financial records to a designated person or entity.

Key purposes:

- Provides trusted individuals access to financial records when needed (e.g., attorney, accountant, family member).
- Allows financial advisors to share information with a spouse, co-trustee, or executor.
- Creates a record of consent to protect institutions

from liability.

Important considerations:

- Authorization should clearly identify both the account holder and the recipient of information.
- Scope should specify which accounts and what type of information may be disclosed.
- The form does not grant transaction authority (unlike a Power of Attorney). It only permits release of information.
- The authorization can be revoked in writing at any time.

Structured outline of a **Financial Information Release Authorization**:

1. **Title and Declaration**
   "Financial Information Release Authorization."
2. **Identification of Account Holder**
   Full name, address, and identifying account numbers.
3. **Authorized Recipient**
   Name and contact details of person(s) allowed to receive information.
4. **Scope of Disclosure**

Types of financial records (balances, statements, tax forms, etc.).

5. **Purpose of Disclosure**
   For legal, tax, accounting, or estate planning purposes.
6. **Expiration**
   Specific date or event that ends authorization.
7. **Revocation Rights**
   Statement that the account holder may revoke at any time by written notice.
8. **Signatures**
   Account holder's signature, with optional witness or notary.

Sample Form Language (for illustration only):

> **FINANCIAL INFORMATION RELEASE AUTHORIZATION**
>
> Account Holder Name: ______________________________ Address: ______________________________
>
> **1. Authorization.** I authorize ______________________________ (financial institution/advisor) to release the following

information:

____

2. Recipient. The information may be provided to: Name:

____

Address/Phone:

____

3. Scope of Disclosure. This authorization applies to the following accounts or records:

____

4. Purpose. The disclosure is authorized for the following purpose:

____________________________.

5. Expiration. This authorization shall expire on _____________ or upon the occurrence of

____________________________.

6. Revocation. I understand that I may revoke this authorization at any time by providing written notice.

Signature of Account Holder:

________________________________ Date:

____

Witness/Notary (if required):

____

Caution: This authorization does not grant the recipient authority to conduct transactions. It only permits release of information as described.

Chapter 27

Form M

This chapter presents a sample **Guardian Nomination Form**. This form allows parents to nominate a guardian to care for their minor children in the event of the parents' death or incapacity. While final appointment is made by a court, this document provides guidance and strong evidence of parental intent.

Key purposes:

- Ensures parents' wishes regarding guardianship are clearly expressed.
- Provides courts with guidance when determining custody.
- Can reduce disputes among relatives by

documenting parental preferences.

Important considerations:

- This is a nomination, not a guarantee — the court retains final authority.
- Successor guardians should be named in case the first nominee cannot serve.
- Parents may limit guardian powers or provide instructions for child-rearing preferences.
- Execution requirements vary by state, often requiring witnesses or notarization.

Structured outline of a **Guardian Nomination Form**:

1. **Title and Declaration**
   "Guardian Nomination Form" or "Nomination of Guardian for Minor Children."
2. **Parent/Guardian Information**
   Full names of parents/legal guardians making the nomination.
3. **Child Identification**
   Full names and dates of birth of each minor child.
4. **Guardian Nominee**
   Name, address, and relationship of the nominated guardian.

5. **Successor Guardian**
   Alternate nominee if the first choice cannot serve.

6. **Special Instructions**
   Preferences or directions for child's upbringing, education, or healthcare.

7. **Signatures and Witnesses**
   Execution by parents, with witness or notary acknowledgment.

Sample Form Language (for illustration only):

GUARDIAN NOMINATION FORM

We, ______________________________ and ______________________________, being the parents/legal guardians of the following minor child(ren):

Child(ren):

____

hereby nominate:

Name of Guardian:

______________________________ Address:

____

Relationship to Child(ren):

____

to serve as guardian of our child(ren) in the event of our death or incapacity.

If the above-named guardian cannot serve, we nominate: Name of Successor Guardian:

____

Special Instructions (optional):

____

Signatures:

Parent/Guardian:

___________________________________ Date:

____

Parent/Guardian:

___________________________________ Date:

____

Witnesses:

____

____

Notary Acknowledgment (if required):

Subscribed and sworn before me this

_______________ day of _______________,

20_____.

Notary Public:

____

Caution: While highly persuasive, courts retain discretion in appointing guardians. Parents should coordinate this form with wills and trusts for consistency.

Chapter 28

Form N

This chapter presents a sample **Beneficiary Designation Form**. This form allows an individual to designate who will receive specific assets — such as retirement accounts, life insurance, or payable-on-death (POD) bank accounts — directly upon death, outside of probate.

Key purposes:

- Directs financial institutions and insurers to transfer assets to named beneficiaries.
- Avoids probate for designated accounts and policies.
- Coordinates with wills and trusts for consistent

estate planning.

Important considerations:

- Each financial institution typically provides its own beneficiary form; this template shows general structure.
- Primary and contingent beneficiaries should be named.
- Percentages of distribution should add up to 100%.
- Beneficiary designations override wills or trusts, so consistency is essential.

Structured outline of a **Beneficiary Designation Form**:

1. **Title and Declaration**
   "Beneficiary Designation Form."
2. **Account or Policy Information**
   Identification of the account, policy, or asset covered.
3. **Account Holder Information**
   Name, address, and signature of the owner.
4. **Primary Beneficiaries**
   Names, addresses, relationships, and percentage shares.

5. **Contingent Beneficiaries**
   Names and shares if primary beneficiaries predecease owner.
6. **Effective Date and Revocation**
   Statement that this designation revokes prior ones.
7. **Signatures and Witnesses**
   Execution by account holder, and witness/notary if required.

Sample Form Language (for illustration only):

BENEFICIARY DESIGNATION FORM

Account/Policy Number:

____

Institution/Company:

____

Account Holder: Name:

______________________________ Address:

____

Primary Beneficiaries:

Name	Relationship	% Share
__________	__________	__________
__________	__________	__________

Contingent Beneficiaries (if primary predecease):

Name	Relationship	% Share
____________	____________	____________

Effective Date and Revocation. This designation revokes any prior beneficiary designations for the above account/policy.

Signature of Account Holder:

________________________________ Date: ______________

Witness/Notary (if required):

____

Caution: Beneficiary designations legally control the transfer of covered assets. Inconsistent designations between accounts and estate documents can create disputes.

Chapter 29

Form O

This chapter provides a sample **Memorandum of Personal Property**. This document is often referenced in a will or trust and allows the owner to leave specific tangible items (such as furniture, jewelry, artwork, or heirlooms) to designated individuals, without amending the will itself.

Key purposes:

- Provides flexibility in distributing household and personal effects.
- Allows changes to be made easily, without executing a new will.
- Reduces family conflict by clarifying the decedent's

wishes.

Important considerations:

- Not all states recognize separate memoranda unless specifically authorized in a will or trust.
- The memorandum should be signed and dated by the owner.
- Only tangible personal property is typically included — not cash, stocks, or real estate.
- Updates should be carefully coordinated to avoid conflicting instructions.

Structured outline of a **Memorandum of Personal Property**:

1. **Title and Declaration**
   "Memorandum of Personal Property" identifying the owner and reference to will or trust.

2. **Owner Information**
   Full name and address of the person making the memorandum.

3. **Itemized Distribution List**
   Specific description of each item and the beneficiary designated to receive it.

4. **Statement of Binding Effect**

Confirmation that the memorandum is intended to be legally binding if permitted by state law.

5. **Signature and Date**
   Execution by the owner.

Sample Form Language (for illustration only):

MEMORANDUM OF PERSONAL PROPERTY

I, ______________________________, residing at ______________________________, make the following designations of my tangible personal property, to be distributed in accordance with my Last Will and Testament or Living Trust.

Itemized Distribution:

Description of Item	Beneficiary
________________	________________
________________	________________
________________	________________

I reserve the right to revoke or amend this memorandum at any time prior to my death.

Signature: ____________________________

Date: ________________

Caution: This memorandum is only effective if recognized by state law and properly referenced in a valid will or trust.

Chapter 30

Form P

This chapter provides a sample **Letter of Intent**. Unlike a will or trust, this document is not legally binding. Instead, it offers guidance, explanations, and personal messages to family members, fiduciaries, or guardians. It is often used to communicate wishes that may not fit neatly into formal legal documents.

Key purposes:

- Provides context for estate planning decisions.
- Offers instructions for guardians on how children should be raised.
- Communicates personal values, traditions, or burial preferences.

- Leaves guidance for managing family-owned businesses or special assets.

Important considerations:

- Because it is not legally binding, the letter should not contradict wills, trusts, or beneficiary designations.
- It may be updated informally as circumstances change.
- Can be stored with estate documents so fiduciaries and family members can access it.
- Tone may be both practical and personal, blending instructions with expressions of love or encouragement.

Structured outline of a **Letter of Intent**:

1. **Title and Heading**
   "Letter of Intent" or "Personal Letter of Instruction."
2. **Identification of Author**
   Name, address, and date.
3. **Family and Guardian Guidance**
   Instructions for care of minor children or dependents.

4. **Personal Messages**
   Words of encouragement, values, traditions, or faith.
5. **Financial and Practical Notes**
   Information on key accounts, contacts, or special assets.
6. **Funeral or Burial Preferences**
   Desired arrangements, if not already included in estate documents.
7. **Closing Statement and Signature**
   Final words and signature of the author.

Sample Form Language (for illustration only):

LETTER OF INTENT

Date: ______________

I, __________________, residing at __________________, write this letter to provide guidance and share my wishes with my loved ones and those who may be responsible for my affairs.

1. Family Guidance. It is my wish that my children, __________________, be raised with love, stability, and in accordance with the values of ____________________. I ask that guardians ensure their education, healthcare, and spiritual needs are met.

2. Personal Messages. I encourage my family to continue our traditions of ____________________, and to remember that my greatest hope is for unity, kindness, and perseverance.

3. Financial and Practical Notes. Important contacts: ____________________. Special assets or items requiring care: ____________________.

4. Funeral or Burial Preferences. My preference is for ____________________.

This letter is written to guide and support those I leave behind. Though not legally binding, I trust it will be received in the spirit of love and responsibility with which it is given.

Signature: ________________________

Note: This document supplements formal estate planning instruments. It should be updated regularly and stored with wills, trusts, and powers of attorney.

Chapter 31

Form Q

This chapter provides a sample **Digital Assets Authorization Form**. This form gives a trusted individual permission to access, manage, and close digital accounts or online property. It addresses modern estate planning concerns about email accounts, cloud storage, social media, digital wallets, and other online assets.

Key purposes:

- Ensures a fiduciary or agent can access and manage online accounts.
- Provides legal consent required under federal and state privacy laws.
- Helps prevent digital assets from being lost, locked,

or abandoned.

- Clarifies how digital property should be handled after death or incapacity.

Important considerations:

- Many states have enacted the *Revised Uniform Fiduciary Access to Digital Assets Act (RUFADAA)*, which governs access.
- Without clear authorization, providers may deny access to accounts.
- The form should specify which accounts, files, or categories of assets are covered.
- A successor agent should be named if the first choice cannot serve.

Structured outline of a **Digital Assets Authorization Form**:

1. **Title and Declaration**
   "Digital Assets Authorization Form."
2. **Identification of Owner**
   Full name and contact information of the account holder.
3. **Authorized Agent**

Name, relationship, and contact information of the trusted agent.

4. **Scope of Authority**
   Permission to access, manage, download, delete, or close accounts.

5. **Accounts and Assets Covered**
   Specific accounts, categories, or "all digital assets."

6. **Successor Agent**
   Alternate representative in case the first cannot serve.

7. **Effective Date and Duration**
   When the authority begins and how long it lasts.

8. **Signatures and Notarization**
   Execution by the owner, with witness or notary acknowledgment.

Sample Form Language (for illustration only):

> **DIGITAL ASSETS AUTHORIZATION FORM**
>
> I, ____________________, authorize the following person to act as my Digital Assets Agent:
>
> Name: ____________________

Address: ____________________

Phone/Email: ____________________

1. Scope of Authority. My Agent is authorized to access, manage, control, delete, download, or close my digital accounts, including but not limited to:

____

2. Accounts Covered. This authorization applies to:
[all digital assets / specific accounts] such as email, social media, online banking, digital wallets, and cloud storage.

3. Successor Agent. If the above-named Agent cannot serve, I appoint:

____________________.

4. Duration. This authorization is effective [immediately / upon my incapacity / upon my death] and remains valid until revoked in writing.

Signature: ________________________

Date: _______________

Witnesses:

____

____

Notary Acknowledgment (if required):
Subscribed and sworn before me this
________________ day of ________________,
20_____.

Notary Public: ____________________________

Caution: Digital access laws differ by state and by provider. This form should be paired with updated estate documents and, where available, provider-specific legacy tools.

Chapter 32

Form R

This chapter provides a sample **Funeral and Burial Instructions Form**. This form allows an individual to state preferences for funeral, burial, or cremation arrangements, helping family members and executors carry out their wishes without confusion or conflict.

Key purposes:

- Provides clear instructions for funeral and memorial arrangements.
- States preferences for burial, cremation, or donation of remains.
- Reduces family disputes by documenting the individual's wishes.

- Offers guidance on religious, cultural, or personal rituals.

Important considerations:

- Some states give priority to written funeral instructions over family decisions.
- The form should be stored with estate planning documents, but not in a safe deposit box (which may be inaccessible at time of death).
- Instructions may include budget preferences, service providers, and choice of cemetery or crematory.
- While not always legally binding, written instructions are usually followed if clearly expressed.

Structured outline of a **Funeral and Burial Instructions Form**:

1. **Title and Declaration**
   "Funeral and Burial Instructions Form."
2. **Personal Identification**
   Full name, address, and date of birth of the individual.
3. **Funeral Arrangements**

Preferences for type of service, location, clergy/celebrant, music, and readings.

4. **Disposition of Remains**
   Burial, cremation, or donation to science, with detailed instructions.

5. **Special Requests**
   Religious, cultural, or family traditions to be honored.

6. **Financial Instructions**
   Prepaid plans, insurance coverage, or budget limits for services.

7. **Signature and Date**
   Execution by the individual, with optional witness or notary.

Sample Form Language (for illustration only):

FUNERAL AND BURIAL INSTRUCTIONS FORM

I, ______________________, residing at ______________________, set forth my wishes regarding funeral and burial arrangements.

1. Funeral Arrangements. Type of service:

[religious / non-religious / memorial only].
Preferred location: ____________________.
Clergy/Celebrant:
_________________________. Other
preferences (music, readings, flowers):
___________________________________.

2. Disposition of Remains. I direct that my remains be:
[buried / cremated / donated to science].
Details (cemetery, urn, scattering location):
___________________________________.

3. Special Requests. I request the following religious, cultural, or family traditions:
____.

4. Financial Instructions. Prepaid arrangements: ____________________.
Insurance or other funding:
____________________. Budget guidance:
____________________.

Signature: _________________________
Date: _______________

Witness/Notary (optional):

____

Caution: This form should be communicated to family and stored in an accessible place. It should not be locked away where it cannot be retrieved promptly at the time of death.

Chapter 33

Form S

This chapter provides a sample **Business Succession Plan Template**. This form allows a business owner to outline what will happen to the business in the event of retirement, incapacity, or death. A written plan ensures continuity, minimizes disruption, and provides guidance for successors, employees, and family members.

Key purposes:

- Establishes who will manage or inherit the business.
- Provides financial arrangements for transfer of ownership.
- Addresses management continuity and employee

stability.

- Reduces disputes among heirs, partners, or co-owners.

Important considerations:

- Plans may involve buy-sell agreements, life insurance funding, or trusts.
- Successor choice should balance family considerations with business competence.
- Tax and legal consequences should be reviewed with professionals.
- Regular review is important to keep the plan aligned with the business's growth and changes.

Structured outline of a **Business Succession Plan Template**:

1. **Title and Declaration**
   "Business Succession Plan."
2. **Owner and Business Information**
   Name of business owner, business name, and description.
3. **Successor Designation**
   Identification of successor(s) to own or manage the business.

4. **Management Continuity**
   Interim management structure in case of sudden incapacity or death.
5. **Transfer of Ownership**
   Terms of transfer (sale, gift, trust transfer, or buy-sell agreement).
6. **Financial Arrangements**
   Funding mechanisms such as insurance or installment payments.
7. **Employee and Customer Communication**
   Instructions for reassuring employees and preserving client relationships.
8. **Review and Update Clause**
   Statement that the plan should be revisited periodically.
9. **Signatures**
   Execution by the owner, with optional witness or notary.

Sample Form Language (for illustration only):

BUSINESS SUCCESSION PLAN

Business Owner: ____________________

Business Name: ____________________

1. Successor Designation. I designate ________________________ as the successor to manage/own my business in the event of my death, incapacity, or retirement.

2. Management Continuity. If immediate succession is not possible, interim management shall be provided by ________________________.

3. Transfer of Ownership. Ownership shall transfer by means of: [sale / gift / trust transfer / buy-sell agreement] under the following terms: ________________________________.

4. Financial Arrangements. The transfer shall be funded through: [life insurance / installment payments].

5. Employee and Customer Communication. The successor shall notify employees, clients, and vendors promptly, assuring them of continuity and stability.

6. Review and Updates. This plan should be reviewed and updated at least every [2 / 5] years or upon significant business changes.

Signature of Business Owner:

________________________________ Date: ______________

Witness/Notary (optional):

____

Caution: Business succession planning often involves complex tax, valuation, and legal issues. Professional guidance is strongly recommended.

Chapter 34

Form T

This chapter provides a sample **Designation of Standby Guardian**. This document allows a parent or legal guardian to designate in advance who should assume guardianship of a minor child in the event of the parent's incapacity or death. It provides continuity of care and reduces uncertainty in court proceedings.

Key purposes:

- Ensures children are placed with a trusted adult chosen by the parent.
- Reduces family disputes and judicial guesswork regarding custody.
- Provides a clear transition of guardianship during

periods of incapacity or after death.

- Allows for naming of both primary and alternate guardians.

Important considerations:

- The designation may require court confirmation to become legally effective.
- Parents should name an alternate in case the primary guardian cannot serve.
- Instructions regarding health, education, or religious upbringing may be included.
- State laws vary on whether the designation must be notarized or witnessed.

Structured outline of a **Designation of Standby Guardian**:

1. **Title and Declaration**
   "Designation of Standby Guardian."
2. **Parent/Guardian Information**
   Full name and address of the designating parent or guardian.
3. **Child(ren) Identification**
   Full names and dates of birth of the minor child(ren).

4. **Primary Guardian Nomination**
   Name, address, and relationship of the standby guardian.

5. **Alternate Guardian**
   Name of an alternate guardian if the first choice cannot serve.

6. **Triggering Events**
   Statement that the designation becomes effective upon incapacity, death, or written designation by parent.

7. **Special Instructions**
   Optional preferences for upbringing or care.

8. **Signatures and Notarization**
   Parent's signature, witness attestation, and notary acknowledgment if required.

Sample Form Language (for illustration only):

> **DESIGNATION OF STANDBY GUARDIAN**
>
> I, ______________________________, residing at ______________________________, being the parent/legal guardian of the following minor child(ren):

Child(ren):

____

do hereby designate:

Primary Standby Guardian:

____

Address: ______________________________

Relationship:

____

If the above-named person cannot serve, I designate:

Alternate Standby Guardian:

____

Address: ______________________________

Relationship:

____

Triggering Events. This designation shall become effective upon my incapacity, death, or written declaration.

Special Instructions (optional):

____

.

Signature of Parent/Guardian:

_________________________ Date:

____

Witnesses:

____

____

Notary Acknowledgment (if required):
Subscribed and sworn before me this
________________ day of ________________,
20_____.

Notary Public: ______________________________

Caution: This designation guides the court but may not be binding. Local statutes should be checked to ensure compliance.

Chapter 35

Form U

This chapter provides a sample **Special Power of Attorney for Childcare**. This document authorizes another adult to make day-to-day decisions for a minor child, usually for a limited time, such as when a parent is traveling, deployed, or otherwise unavailable.

Key purposes:

- Grants authority to a caregiver for school enrollment, medical care, and daily needs.
- Avoids disruption of the child's routine when a parent is temporarily absent.
- Provides legal recognition of the caregiver's authority.

- Can specify duration and scope of authority.

Important considerations:

- This power of attorney does not permanently transfer guardianship.
- Duration should be clearly stated (e.g., six months, one year).
- Scope may be broad or limited (medical, educational, financial).
- State laws vary; some require notarization or limit the maximum effective period.

Structured outline of a **Special Power of Attorney for Childcare**:

1. **Title and Declaration**
   "Special Power of Attorney for Childcare."
2. **Parent/Guardian Information**
   Full name and address of the parent granting authority.
3. **Child(ren) Identification**
   Full names and dates of birth of minor child(ren).
4. **Attorney-in-Fact (Caregiver)**
   Name, address, and relationship of the designated caregiver.

5. **Scope of Authority**
   Specific powers granted (medical, educational, financial, daily care).

6. **Duration**
   Start and end dates of the authorization.

7. **Limitations**
   Any restrictions on the powers granted.

8. **Signatures and Notarization**
   Execution by the parent, with witness or notary acknowledgment as required.

Sample Form Language (for illustration only):

> **SPECIAL POWER OF ATTORNEY FOR CHILDCARE**
>
> I, ____________________, residing at ____________________, being the parent/legal guardian of:
>
> Child(ren): ______________________________
>
> hereby appoint:
>
> Name of Caregiver: ______________________________ Address: ______________________________

Relationship:

____

as my true and lawful attorney-in-fact to make decisions regarding the care of my child(ren).

1. Scope of Authority. The caregiver is authorized to:

- Consent to medical and dental treatment.
- Enroll the child(ren) in school and authorize school-related activities.
- Provide for housing, food, clothing, and daily care.
- Manage financial matters directly related to the child(ren)'s welfare.

2. Duration. This authorization shall begin on _______________ and end on _______________, unless revoked earlier in writing.

3. Limitations. This power does not grant authority to permanently transfer guardianship or to consent to adoption.

Signature of Parent/Guardian:

____________________________ Date: ________________

Witnesses:

____

____

Notary Acknowledgment (if required):
Subscribed and sworn before me this ________________ day of ________________, 20_____.

Notary Public: ____________________________

Caution: This form is intended for temporary delegation. Long-term or permanent arrangements usually require a guardianship order from a court.

Chapter 36

Working with Lawyers

One of the first questions nearly everyone asks when they first hear about trusts is: "Do I need a lawyer for this?" The honest answer is: it depends. A trust is a powerful legal tool, but it does not come in a one-size-fits-all package. The complexity of your life—your family, your finances, your property, and even your state's laws—determines whether you can safely set one up on your own or whether professional help is a must.

This chapter is about navigating that choice with confidence. We will examine when a do-it-yourself (DIY) trust might work, when it becomes risky, how to find and evaluate attorneys, what to watch out for in online services, and how to blend these approaches if you want the best of both worlds. Along the way, we'll also look at common red flags and give you questions to ask so you can spot value versus snake oil.

36.1 When DIY is Fine vs. When It's Risky

Do-it-yourself estate planning has exploded in popularity. Online kits, downloadable templates, and even phone apps promise quick, cheap ways to create a trust. And sometimes, they deliver exactly that. If your situation is simple—say, you are married, own a single home, have a few accounts, and want everything divided equally among your spouse and children—a DIY trust may be enough to meet your goals. In such cases, the main purpose of the trust is to avoid probate and streamline inheritance. The rules are straightforward, and the margin for error is relatively small.

But the moment complexity enters the picture, DIY becomes risky. Complexity comes in many forms:

- **Blended families.** If you have stepchildren, multiple marriages, or a partner outside of marriage, clear instructions are crucial. DIY kits rarely capture the nuance required to balance these interests.

- **High-value or diverse assets.** Owning multiple properties, business interests, or investment portfolios adds layers of tax and legal issues. Templates often overlook these.
- **Special needs beneficiaries.** If a child or dependent receives government benefits, the wrong wording could disqualify them from assistance. Specialized drafting is essential.
- **Desire for control.** If you want staggered distributions, conditions on inheritance, or asset protection provisions, off-the-shelf documents may not provide the needed detail.

The risk with DIY is not just mistakes in wording—it is the silent gaps you may never notice. A trust that looks fine on paper can fail when put to the test. Courts may invalidate provisions, banks may refuse to honor them, or family members may find loopholes. At that point, the money saved upfront is lost many times over in legal fees and disputes.

36.2 Shopping for an Attorney

If you decide to seek professional help, the next challenge is finding the right attorney. Not every lawyer handles estate planning, and even fewer specialize in trusts.

Hiring the wrong lawyer is almost as dangerous as going without one. Here are some tips for choosing wisely:

- **Look for a specialist.** Estate planning is its own field. Ask whether the lawyer routinely drafts trusts and whether they are familiar with your state's specific rules.
- **Ask about fees.** Some lawyers charge hourly, while others offer flat fees for standard documents. A flat fee is often better for peace of mind, since you know the cost upfront.
- **Evaluate communication.** A good lawyer explains concepts in plain English. If they cannot make you understand your own trust, that is a red flag.
- **Request transparency.** Ask for a written engagement letter spelling out exactly what is included—drafting, notary services, revisions, and follow-up advice.

Treat the process like hiring any professional. You would not hire a contractor without checking references or a mechanic without asking questions. Estate planning is no different. A competent attorney will welcome your questions and respect your concerns.

36.3 Online Kits and Red Flags

Online trust kits can be helpful—but the marketplace is full of both gems and scams. Some services tailor documents by state, offer step-by-step questionnaires, and provide customer support. Others churn out generic forms with little regard for compliance. To evaluate them:

- **Promises too good to be true.** Beware of claims like "guaranteed to save taxes" or "works in every state." Trust law is state-specific, and no kit is universally perfect.
- **Ultra-low pricing.** While affordability is a benefit, a $29 kit that claims to cover every scenario is likely overselling itself. You often get what you pay for.
- **Lack of support.** A reliable service offers customer service, explanations, and perhaps even attorney review. If support is absent, caution is warranted.
- **Outdated documents.** Laws change. If the kit hasn't been updated in years, it may contain provisions that are no longer valid.

Online kits can be fine for very simple cases, especially if you supplement them with your own research. But remember: these companies often sell peace of mind, not actual legal protection. The burden of accuracy remains on you.

36.4 The Hybrid Approach

One increasingly popular method is to combine the best of both worlds. Draft a trust using an online platform, then hire an attorney to review it for accuracy. This "hybrid approach" has several advantages:

- Lower cost than full-service legal drafting.
- Faster turnaround—many online platforms can generate a draft in hours.
- Professional oversight ensures compliance with state law and corrects common mistakes.

Imagine it like doing your taxes with software, then paying a CPA to review before filing. You save time and money but still gain professional assurance. Many attorneys now offer flat-fee reviews for this exact purpose.

36.5 Beyond the Basics

Lawyers can offer more than just drafting documents. They can:

- Suggest tax-saving strategies if your estate is large.
- Coordinate with financial advisors to align your investments with your estate plan.
- Draft specialized provisions for unique assets, such as intellectual property, rental businesses, or foreign property.
- Represent your trustees after your death, helping them administer the trust efficiently.

If you have complex goals—such as protecting assets from creditors, providing for a child with disabilities, or balancing a blended family—lawyers can craft provisions that DIY kits will never include. This extra layer of strategy is often worth the investment.

36.6 Case Examples

To illustrate, consider two examples:

- **DIY Success.** A couple with one home, two children, and modest savings used an online kit to create a revocable living trust. They funded it properly, transferred the home, and updated bank accounts. When one spouse died, the surviving spouse managed everything smoothly without probate. The trust did exactly what they wanted.

- **DIY Failure.** Another family with a blended household used a free trust template they found online. It did not account for stepchildren. After their death, the surviving spouse inherited everything, leaving the children from the first marriage with nothing. The result: years of litigation and a fractured family. The trust technically existed—but it failed its purpose.

These stories show that DIY is not inherently bad, but context matters. The difference is not the document alone, but whether it fits the family's reality.

36.7 Takeaway

Lawyers are not always necessary, but sometimes they are invaluable. The key is to match the tool to the task. For simple estates, a DIY trust or hybrid model may be sufficient. For complex estates, professional help is worth every penny. Online kits can provide a starting point but must be chosen carefully. The spectrum is wide—from free downloads to high-end legal services—and the right choice depends on your needs, not on marketing promises.

The most important thing is this: do not let fear of cost or complexity prevent you from acting. A mediocre trust is better than no plan at all. But a well-crafted trust, guided by the right professionals when needed, can save your family enormous time, money, and conflict. Know yourself, know your estate, and choose wisely.

Chapter 37

Miscellaneous Topics

Some of the most important elements of estate planning do not fit neatly into single categories like wills, trusts, or powers of attorney. They cross boundaries, blending financial, legal, and personal decisions into strategies that protect families, reduce risks, and preserve legacies. This chapter gathers those "miscellaneous but essential" topics—practical issues that, if overlooked, can undermine even the best-intentioned plan. Each section is written plainly, with an eye toward preventing mistakes and creating durable, flexible outcomes.

37.1 Bulletproof Living Trusts

A living trust is only as strong as its drafting. To be "bulletproof," it must:

- Clearly identify the grantor, trustee(s), and beneficiaries.
- Use unambiguous language regarding distributions, contingencies, and successor trustees.
- Include provisions for incapacity and successor management.
- Contain "spendthrift" clauses to protect beneficiaries from creditors.
- Comply with state-specific rules for execution and validity.

The more precisely your trust reflects your goals—whether providing staged inheritances, supporting a disabled child, or blending families—the harder it is to challenge.

37.2 Seven Deadly Mistakes

Estate plans often fail for predictable reasons:

1. Failing to fund the trust.

2. Choosing the wrong trustee or executor.
3. Using DIY forms without legal review.
4. Neglecting to update documents after life changes.
5. Overlooking tax consequences.
6. Ignoring digital assets.
7. Assuming "equal" always means "fair" in blended families.

Even seasoned professionals sometimes miss these traps. Awareness is prevention.

37.3 Minimizing Taxes

For most households, the federal estate tax is not an issue due to high exemptions. But for high-net-worth families:

- Gifting strategies, such as annual exclusion gifts, reduce the taxable estate.
- Irrevocable life insurance trusts (ILITs) keep death benefits outside the estate.
- Charitable remainder trusts or donor-advised funds align philanthropy with tax efficiency.
- Proper valuation of closely held businesses prevents

inflated assessments.

The goal is legal minimization—reducing taxes without triggering IRS scrutiny.

37.4 Asset Protection Strategies

Your plan should anticipate risks from creditors, lawsuits, or divorce:

- Use of LLCs or family limited partnerships for business or rental properties.
- Homestead protections (especially strong in Florida).
- Prenuptial agreements for second marriages.
- Spendthrift clauses in trusts.

Proper structuring keeps assets insulated while maintaining family control.

37.5 Out of Probate

Probate drains time and money. The key to avoiding it is:

- Funding living trusts with all major assets.
- Using payable-on-death (POD) and

transfer-on-death (TOD) designations.

- Titling property jointly with survivorship when appropriate.

Each measure shifts assets outside the probate process, ensuring faster, quieter transfers.

37.6 Funding Trusts Correctly

A trust without assets is an empty box. Proper funding requires:

- Recording new deeds transferring real estate into the trust.
- Retitling bank and brokerage accounts.
- Updating life insurance and retirement account beneficiary designations.

Funding must be ongoing, not a one-time event.

37.7 Charitable Giving

Charity can be embedded into your estate plan through:

- Specific bequests in a will or trust.
- Charitable trusts that provide tax benefits.
- Naming charities as life insurance or retirement

account beneficiaries.

This ensures your legacy extends beyond family, aligning wealth with values.

37.8 Updating Your Plan

Laws change, families change, and finances change. Estate plans must evolve. Best practices:

- Review every three to five years.
- Update after major life events: marriage, divorce, birth, death, or large purchases.
- Keep documents consistent across trusts, wills, POAs, and beneficiary designations.

37.9 Building Blocks

Most plans must address:

- Property ownership and transfer.
- Fiduciary appointments (trustees, executors, guardians).
- Medical decision-making (advance directives).
- Financial authority during incapacity (POAs).

Skipping these basics undermines everything else.

37.10 Incapacity

To ensure your voice is heard if you cannot speak:

- Draft durable financial POAs.
- Appoint health care surrogates.
- Complete living wills or advance directives.
- Consider HIPAA releases for medical privacy.

These tools avoid court guardianships and maintain dignity.

37.11 Digital Asset Protection

Modern estates include:

- Cryptocurrency and digital wallets.
- Online bank and brokerage accounts.
- Cloud storage, photos, and personal data.
- Social media accounts.

Plans should include access instructions, account inventories, and trusted digital fiduciaries.

37.12 Cross-Border Planning

If you own property abroad or are not a U.S. citizen:

- Be aware of foreign inheritance laws.
- Coordinate wills and trusts across jurisdictions.
- Consider tax treaties and reporting obligations.

Ignoring cross-border issues can lead to double taxation or unintended heirs.

37.13 Special Needs

Special care is needed for second marriages, stepchildren, or disabled beneficiaries:

- Use trusts to ensure children from prior marriages are protected.
- Avoid outright gifts to special needs children that jeopardize benefits; use special needs trusts.
- Communicate intentions clearly to reduce disputes.

37.14 Business Succession

Business owners need exit strategies:

- Buy-sell agreements funded with insurance.
- Grooming successors or co-owners.
- Using trusts or LLCs to maintain continuity.

Without planning, businesses often collapse after the founder's death or incapacity.

37.15 Assembling the Team

Even the best documents fail without the right people:

- **Trustees:** Must be reliable, organized, and impartial.
- **Executors:** Should have patience and administrative skill.
- **Attorneys and Advisors:** Specialists in estate planning, tax, and financial management.

The team makes the plan workable.

37.16 Guiding Estate Administration

After death, administration requires:

- Gathering and valuing assets.
- Paying debts and taxes.
- Communicating regularly with beneficiaries.
- Distributing assets according to instructions.

Good planning reduces confusion, while clear instructions minimize conflict.

37.17 Takeaway

Estate planning is not just about signing a few documents. It is about weaving together trusts, wills, POAs, health care instructions, and financial structures in a way that survives challenges, avoids court entanglements, and reflects your goals. The topics in this chapter highlight the "extra" steps that separate fragile plans from durable ones. Attention to these details—funding, updating, digital access, family dynamics, taxes, and succession—ensures that your plan works in real life, not just on paper.

Chapter 38

30-Day Plan

Creating a trust may feel like climbing a mountain—distant, intimidating, and only for those with special equipment. But the truth is, with a clear map and steady pacing, you can reach the summit in thirty days. The key is to take it week by week, breaking a big project into manageable steps. By the end of the month, you will not just have a signed document—you will have a funded, functioning trust that your family can rely on when it matters most.

This chapter offers a roadmap. Think of it as a guided hike: each week has a focus, examples to help you picture the process, and checklists to keep you on track. You don't need to do everything at once. You just need to keep moving forward.

38.1 Clerks, Judges, and Reality

Before diving into the timeline, a practical note: the legal system is not just rules on paper—it is people. Clerk's offices are the gatekeepers of filings. Their policies and preferences may differ dramatically from city to city, county to county, and state to state. One office may happily accept a two-page filing stapled in the upper left corner; another may reject it unless it is bound a certain way or accompanied by a cover sheet.

Do not overlook the human factor. Establishing a courteous, even friendly relationship with deputy clerks can be invaluable. They often decide, in real time, whether your paperwork looks "in order." Giving them what they are accustomed to—and respecting their role—can prevent needless rejections and delays.

The same applies with judges. While judges decide matters based on law, the legal system is also premised on familiarity, consistency, and professional decorum. Approaching judges with respect, never condescension or hostility, is essential. A bit of finesse goes a long way: their discretion can directly affect whether filings are managed smoothly or bogged down.

Bottom line: never be disrespectful to a deputy clerk or a judge. Their cooperation can make or break the efficiency of your filings.

Disclaimer: I am an attorney, but nothing in this book creates an attorney–client relationship between me and you, the reader. This is an educational resource only. Laws differ by state, county, and even city. Practices change. Court dynamics vary. What is routine in one jurisdiction may be unusual in another. You must do your own homework, exercise independent thought, and apply judgment to your situation. Do not treat this book as a substitute for personalized legal advice.

38.2 Dealing with Other Entities

Filing documents with the court is only part of the process. At some point you may need to present your trust, power of attorney, healthcare directive, or other forms to banks, insurance companies, hospitals, doctors, or similar institutions. These entities often serve as gatekeepers in their own right.

Be mindful that:

- Each institution has its own internal policies, compliance departments, and legal counsel. What one branch accepts without issue, another may refuse.

- Staff at banks or hospitals may not be trained in the nuances of estate planning law, but they may have strict checklists that you will need to satisfy.
- Even when the law is on your side, the process may still stall because the institution fears liability or has been advised by in-house attorneys to "say no" first.

Just as with clerks and judges, respect and courtesy matter. A cooperative relationship with a banker, insurance representative, or healthcare provider can make things much smoother. Patience and professionalism often open doors more effectively than threats or demands.

That said, if you hit a true roadblock—if an institution becomes unreasonable or refuses to follow proper procedures—consider formal avenues of redress. Options include:

- Filing complaints with federal regulators such as the **Consumer Financial Protection Bureau (CFPB)** for financial institutions.
- Seeking recourse through federal or state agencies that regulate banks, insurers, or credit unions.

- Contacting state licensing boards that oversee healthcare providers, hospitals, and medical professionals.
- Consulting with private legal counsel if the matter escalates beyond what informal resolution can achieve.

The takeaway: Develop good relationships with institutional gatekeepers. Do your best to work within their systems. But remember, you are not powerless. Oversight bodies exist to ensure fair treatment, and you have the right to pursue remedies if you are treated unfairly or stonewalled.

38.3 Week 1

The first week is all about education and preparation. Before you can build anything, you need to know the materials you are working with.

- Start by reading about trusts—the earlier chapters of this book are a solid foundation. If something feels unclear, write it down. Those notes will become the questions you ask an attorney or financial advisor later.
- Make a complete list of what you own: your home, any additional property, bank accounts, retirement

accounts, life insurance policies, vehicles, businesses, and even valuable personal items like jewelry or art.

- Identify how each asset is currently titled. Is the house in your name alone? Joint tenancy with a spouse? Payable-on-death to a child? These details determine how easily each item can move into a trust.
- Write down the names of the people you care about most—spouse, children, grandchildren, siblings, or charities. This list becomes your initial "beneficiary brainstorm."

By the end of week one, you should have a snapshot of your financial life. Think of it as laying all your puzzle pieces on the table before you begin assembling them. The picture will be much clearer when everything is in view.

38.4 Week 2

Week two is decision time. With your assets and priorities in front of you, you now decide on the type of trust. For most people, this will be a revocable living trust. It gives you control while you are alive and flexibility to make changes as life evolves.

Next comes drafting. Here are your options:

- Use an online service for a simple estate with straightforward beneficiaries.
- Hire an attorney if you have a blended family, own a business, or anticipate conflicts.
- Consider a hybrid approach—draft online, then pay for an attorney to review it for accuracy.

When drafting, clarity is everything. Be precise about how assets should be divided. Instead of "my children share equally," specify whether you mean equal dollar amounts or equal percentages of what remains. Decide whether children inherit outright or in stages. State how property should be used in the event of incapacity. Each detail you clarify now is one less decision your family has to argue about later.

By the end of week two, you should have a working draft of your trust. It does not need to be perfect, but it should reflect your values and priorities. Think of it as the framework of a house—walls up, roof on, ready for finishing touches.

38.5 Week 3

Week three is about confirming the people who will carry your plan forward. Start by revisiting your list of possible trustees. Remember, a trustee is not a ceremonial figure—they are a manager. Call or meet with the people you are considering. Ask:

- Are you willing to serve as trustee if I cannot?
- Do you understand the responsibility involved?
- Would you be comfortable asking for professional help if needed?

It is better to have these conversations now than to surprise someone later. Many people assume their oldest child is the obvious choice, only to discover that child feels overwhelmed and would prefer a sibling or professional trustee take the role.

Do the same with your beneficiaries. Double-check that your list reflects your true wishes. Have there been births, adoptions, or marriages since you last thought about this? Do you want to include charitable organizations? The trust should reflect today's reality, not yesterday's assumptions.

Once the cast is set, finalize the document. Sign it in accordance with your state's requirements, typically in front of a notary. Store the original in a safe place. Make at least one copy for yourself and one for your trustee. If you hired an attorney, they may also keep a copy in their files.

By the end of week three, your trust should be complete, signed, and legally valid. At this point, you've built the house and installed the doors. Next week, you move in.

38.6 Week 4

A trust without assets is an empty box. The fourth week is where most people drop the ball—but it is also where your planning comes alive. Funding the trust means changing the legal ownership of your property from you, as an individual, to you as trustee of your trust.

- For real estate, this means recording a new deed transferring the property into the trust's name—usually filed with the clerk's office. Here is where local practice matters: some clerks want cover letters, others want forms attached, and some simply want a clean deed and fee. Know your clerk's rules and approach with respect.
- For bank accounts, this means retitling the accounts or opening new ones in the trust's name.
- For retirement accounts and life insurance, this

often means updating beneficiary designations so they flow into the trust (or directly to individuals, depending on your plan).

- For personal property, you may need a simple assignment form transferring ownership into the trust.

Each transfer creates continuity. Without it, your heirs may still face probate for assets left outside the trust. Picture packing up a moving truck: unless you load the furniture, the house you bought won't feel like home. Funding is loading the truck.

Once the trust is funded, inform your successor trustees where to find the documents and provide them with a simple "letter of instruction." While not legally binding, this letter can explain your reasoning, your values, and any personal notes you want to pass along. It humanizes the legalese and helps trustees carry out your wishes in the spirit you intended.

38.7 Checklist

By the end of thirty days, you should have:

- A signed, valid trust document.
- A clear record of your assets and how they are

titled.

- Trustees confirmed and willing to serve.
- Beneficiaries clearly identified and up to date.
- Deeds, accounts, and designations transferred or assigned to the trust.
- Copies of the trust stored securely, with instructions given to successors.

But this is not the finish line. Estate planning is a living process. Life will change—marriages, divorces, new children, new property. Commit to reviewing your trust every few years or after major life events. Think of it as regular maintenance, like changing the oil in your car. The initial work gets you on the road; the upkeep keeps you moving.

38.8 Takeaway

In thirty days, you can move from uncertainty to confidence. This plan is not theoretical—it is practical, step-by-step, and realistic. It turns estate planning from something people postpone indefinitely into something you can accomplish in a single month.

But remember: courts, clerks, and judges are human beings who operate within systems that vary widely by location. Respect them, learn their ways, and you will find the process smoother. At the same time, this book is not legal advice. You must think independently, do your own research, and when needed, seek professional guidance.

With a trust in place, your family gains security, clarity, and peace of mind. More than that, you gain the satisfaction of knowing you did the work now so that your loved ones won't have to later. That is the true gift a trust provides.

www.ingramcontent.com/pod-product-compliance
Lightning Source LLC
LaVergne TN
LVHW052247200926
848481LV00002B/304
* 9 7 9 8 2 3 2 9 6 0 1 4 8 *